W9-DED-041

Managing
Change

with
Business
Process
Simulation

David Profozich

To join a Prentice Hall PTR Internet mailing list, point to:
http://www.prenhall.com/mail_lists

Prentice Hall PTR
Upper Saddle River, NJ 07458

ISBN 0-13-905837-0

90000

9 780139 058370

Library of Congress Cataloging-in-Publication Data

Profozich, David M.

    Managing change with business process simulation / David M. Profozich

        p.   cm.

    Includes index.

    ISBN 0-13-905837-0

    1. Industrial management--Computer simulation. 2. Decision support systems. 3. Organizational change. I. Title.

HD30.2.P757   1997

658.4'06'0113--dc21   97-30380

                                         CIP

Editorial/production supervision: *Craig Little*
Cover design director: *Jerry Votta*
Cover design: *Peter A. Kauffman*
Manufacturing manager: *Julia Meehan*
Acquisitions editor: *Russ Hall*
Marketing manager: *Miles Williams*

 © 1998 by Prentice Hall PTR
Prentice-Hall, Inc.
A Simon & Schuster Company
Upper Saddle River, New Jersey 07458

Prentice Hall books are widely used by corporations and government agencies for training, marketing, and resale.

The publisher offers discounts on this book when ordered in bulk quantities. For more information, contact Corporate Sales Department, Phone: 800-382-3419; Fax: 201- 236-7141; email: corpsales@prenhall.com or write: Prentice Hall PTR, Corporate Sales Dept., One Lake Street, Upper Saddle River, NJ 07458.

Printed in the United States of America
10 9 8 7 6 5 4 3 2 1

ISBN 0-13-905837-0

Prentice-Hall International (UK) Limited, *London*
Prentice-Hall of Australia Pty. Limited, *Sydney*
Prentice-Hall Canada Inc., *Toronto*
Prentice-Hall Hispanoamericana, S.A., *Mexico*
Prentice-Hall of India Private Limited, *New Delhi*
Prentice-Hall of Japan, Inc., *Tokyo*
Simon & Schuster Asia Pte. Ltd., *Singapore*
Editora Prentice-Hall do Brasil, Ltda., *Rio de Janeiro*

Trademarks

AutoCAD is a registered trademark of Autodesk. TurboTax and TurboTax Business are registered trademarks of Intuit, Inc. Freelance and Lotus 123 are registered trademarks of Lotus Development Corporation. SimCity is a registered trademark of Maxis. FlowCharter is a registered trademark of Micrografx, Inc. ActiveX is a trademark and PowerPoint, Windows, Windows 95, Windows NT, and Visual Basic for Applications are registered trademarks of Microsoft Corporation. Arena is a registered trademark of Systems Modeling Corporation. Visio is a registered trademark of Visio Corporation.

All other trademarks and registered trademarks are acknowledged as being the property of their respective owners.

For my wife and best friend, Linda, who not only puts up with my frenetic life but who also champions my cause.

Contents

Foreword

Since the beginning of time, man has sought to change the world for the better. However, as our technology has advanced, our systems have become more complex, and the consequences of change have become more difficult to analyze. Additionally, many of today's ideas for changing and improving the world are both time consuming and costly to implement. As a result, we require reliable and accurate methods for testing out these ideas before making a large investment in time and money. This is the case whether we are trying to design better transportation, communication, or manufacturing systems—or trying to find better ways to deliver a service.

Simulation is a tool that we use to predict performance and to understand the impact of change. It offers many important and well-recognized benefits. It allows us to test out system designs before they are built, and it reduces the risk and time associated with implementing new systems or changing existing ones. To those familiar with the technology, it is inconceivable that any significant new system would be designed and built, or any existing system significantly modified, without the benefit of simulation.

Although its use has grown over the past 40 years, major investments still are being made in new or modified systems without benefiting from the predictive power of simulation. Sometimes these systems lack the initial capacity that their designers intended, and they must be modified after they are built. Certainly this is costly and time consuming and can cause significant delays in bringing new systems online. However, a more common occurrence—often done unconsciously to avoid the risk and cost of having too little capacity—is to design systems with excess capacity. Although these oversized systems initially perform up to specification, they make inefficient use of resources and are far more costly than they need to be. A simulation study often can save significant capital resources by removing the risk factor and allowing the designers to size the system properly and uniformly to meet the requirements.

The book on simulation that you are holding has been in the making for many years. Its genesis goes back 40 years, before Dave Profozich, the author of this book, became an integral part of this growing simulation industry. The foundations were laid when the first researchers and users developed and applied simulation technology to predict the performance of their new or changed systems. Since then, thousands of researchers, developers, and (most importantly) talented users have been weaving together a fabric of knowledge, tools, and application experiences bringing this technology to the point where it is poised for sustained and rapid growth into the broad-base market. Up until now, however, this fabric has lacked one very important thread—a book that explains the concepts, benefits, and methods of this emerging technology in a clear and concise way to the broad base of nontechnical readers. That is precisely the role of this book.

It is only appropriate that Dave Profozich be the one to add this important thread to the simulation technology fabric. He has spent over a decade analyzing the simulation market and communicating the benefits of this technology to an ever-expanding audience. He is well acquainted with simulation users in a broad cross section of industries and applications. He is an excellent communicator and spokesman for the technology. In addition, he has been an integral part of the growth and success of this industry.

It is also only appropriate that this book be written at this time. Simulation tools have evolved over the past 40 years from rudimentary language-based modeling systems to very powerful and flexible graphics-based simulation and animation environments. The tools are becoming dramatically easier to learn and use, thereby lowering

the barrier to new users. Ease of use, along with the widespread availability of powerful personal computers, has led to the rapid expansion of simulation technology in enterprises throughout the world.

The application domain of simulation also is expanding rapidly.
In the past, the most dramatic changes in enterprises occurred on
the factory floor. Today, change is occurring in all parts of an enterprise. Entire business processes are being revamped to leverage the
explosion in communication and computer technologies. People
throughout the enterprise are facing the challenge of predicting the
performance of new and changing systems.

Dave's purpose here is to bridge the gap between the simulation-
specialist and the many pragmatic, nontechnical analysts who need to
understand and use this technology to solve real problems. He begins
by explaining the core concepts of simulation—including random
processes and abstract models—in terms of simple everyday experiences. He then draws on his own vast experience in the industry to
discuss in detail the compelling benefits of simulation technology.

Dave focuses next on the transition of simulation from a highly
specialized technology to one that is widely used by business analysts and engineers as part of their standard suite of tools. He ana-
lyzes the barriers that this technology presents to the pragmatic,
nontechnical user and shows how these barriers are falling to the
rapid pace of simulation-technology development. He supplements
his analysis with personal testimonials from managers and engineers
in some of the leading companies throughout the world. He also
shows how this technology relates to and augments neighboring
technologies, such as optimization, spreadsheets, and static flowcharts.

In closing, he presents a strategy for implementing simulation
and offers a vision for the future of the market. His suggested implementation strategy is founded on observations of many successes and
failures over the years. As a seasoned champion of this technology, he
understands its limits as well as the keys to making it successful in a
wide range of applications and enterprises.

This book about the emergence of simulation technology into the mass market is in itself an important element in that emergence. Dave brings simulation technology to the pragmatic, nontechnical user in a way that is understandable and compelling. In doing so, he is not only describing the emergence of simulation technology, but he is also playing a critical role in the emergence that he describes.

C. Dennis Pegden
CEO/President, Systems Modeling Corporation

Introduction

The art of progress is to preserve order amid change and to preserve change amid order.

ALFRED NORTH WHITEHEAD

When I began my career in the simulation industry 10 years ago, I shared the belief that some managers in the corporate world still maintain today—that business process simulation is exciting, compelling, even fun. . . but hard to use and often more trouble than it's worth. Over the years, I've heard stories about the rise and fall of exciting, yet complex technologies such as neural networks and artificial intelligence. At times I wondered if the technology that I had bet the early part of my career on would fall into the same abyss that these did.

In 1996—after nine years of wishful thinking and hard selling—I became absolutely convinced that business process simulation would emerge as a technology for the mainstream. And now that is exactly what is happening. Companies all over the world are making strategic investments in business process simulation. Companies in all industries ranging from electronics to warehousing to fast-food restaurants are making it a key part of their planning methodology. The world's premiere management consulting firms are also positioning business process simulation within their technology arsenals. Many software companies are launching new products in this market. And while dramatic advances in business process simulation-software technology have accompanied many complementary advances

1

in information technology, the basic ideas that established this market as a successful small niche decades ago prevail today as business process simulation approaches the mainstream business analyst.

This book was written for the business manager or business analyst who wants to understand those ideas that are central to business process simulation. Perhaps you have been aware of the technology for years but have never completely understood it. Maybe you are considering making business process simulation part of the way you manage your business. Or possibly you have heard that your competitor is using the technology and you would like a sneak peek at what it is all about. If you desire a complete perspective on this exciting technology, you have come to the right place.

From the day I began writing, I maintained that I would write a book about this sophisticated technology that was easy to read— the kind of book that a business professional could complete during a single business trip. I hope you will conclude that I have achieved this goal. At times, I may take you a bit deeper than you would like, but I do so to give you an appropriate foundation, so that your perspective on business process simulation is well rounded and technically valid. You will read much more about what simulation can do rather than about how the technology works internally—though I've sprinkled in a bit of the latter to do justice to the science of business process simulation.

◼ What Type of Simulation?

Before going on, let me clarify something. Various types of simulation technology exist in the world today. In fact, you may already own a copy of simulation technology in your home. SimCity®, the popular game from Maxis that sells for less than $35, allows you and your children to build and manage a new metropolis. You are given a plot of barren land to zone into industrial, residential, and commercial areas where people work, live, and play. After you lay roads, subways, highways, and railroads, you can "simulate" your city—

watching it grow as citizens populate it. Albeit interesting, this is not the kind of simulation technology that has motivated this book.

Other forms of simulation are also outside the scope of this book. For example, flight simulators used by pilots to develop their flying skills are not part of my definition of simulation. Neither is the simulation technology that is used to understand the development and growth of markets and the behaviors of its consumers. In the process industries, chemical simulators that capture such information as heat exchange and the behavior of various control valves are also outside the domain of this book, as are various other simulation tools used to study robotics, kinematics, and ergonomics at a machine or operator cell level.

In financial markets, analysts on Wall Street have been using for many years a technology known as monte carlo simulation to study the behavior of stock prices. Monte carlo simulation is also used by physicists to study surface roughness and kinetic ordering. It was used by the father of the hydrogen bomb (Edward Teller) to study the atmospheric effect of nuclear weapons. Reportedly, there was some early concern that the "H-bomb" might ignite the nitrogen in the world's atmosphere, extinguishing all life in a worldwide firestorm. Simulation showed that the concern was unfounded. While monte carlo simulation has some similarities to the technology that I write about here, it is clearly in a class of its own.

Still another form of simulation that has gained some acceptance in the business and academic worlds is continuous simulation. Continuous simulation is used to represent systems whose state changes continuously over time, such as environmental systems, the level of water in a reservoir, or the temperature of an ingot in a furnace. Again, this form of simulation—although occasionally used in an integrated fashion with the subject matter of this book—is not my motivation.

This book focuses on the type of simulation some people refer to as business process simulation or discrete-event simulation. ("Discrete-event" implies that events occur at specific discrete times as a result of other events.) This technology allows organizations to create computer models of existing or proposed systems in order to study their performance. Using these models, analysts conduct "what-if" scenarios in order to determine the best possible way to implement a business application. Thereby they save companies millions of dollars by helping them identify the best ways to manufacture products, deliver superior customer service, configure warehouses, and design telecommunications systems. This approach has wide application in many industries in both manufacturing and service sectors.

According to *Reengineering the Corporation* (Hammer and Champy, 1993), the real power of information technology is not that it can make the old processes work better, but that it enables organizations to break old rules and create new ways of working—that is, to reengineer. Business process simulation technology enables organizations to engineer and reengineer business processes effectively. It allows them to think "outside the box" to determine new ways to run a business. Business scenarios that differ dramatically can be easily explored and compared with a computerized model.

As the market for simulation grows, business professionals are coining various terms for the emerging technology. As you might expect from the title of this book, I formally prefer to call it business process simulation. Others refer to it as dynamic modeling, process modeling, or process mapping. For simplicity sake throughout the remainder of the book, I will stick to the simple "handle" of *simulation* since it clearly serves the purpose well.

▪ Why Should You Use Simulation?

As the cover title suggests, you should use simulation technology to manage change. Chances are you are working for a company that invests in new facilities, new equipment, and new processes. In the past, you may have used some form of information technology, such as a spreadsheet or CAD (computer-aided design) tool, to aid in managing business process changes. These changes may have taken the form of facility upgrades, consolidations, or new process design. However, you may have never used a tool that truly allows you to capture the dynamics of your business environment in a flexible, breakable, changeable model. Simulation allows you to do exactly that.

By using simulation to manage change, you should ultimately realize the most significant benefits that any information technology can deliver—dramatic improvements in business performance and profitability. Each business scenario that you evaluate offers its own cost-for-performance alternative. You can rule out alternatives that do not meet your business objectives, and you can explore tradeoffs in your implementation strategies in terms of their effect on your overall profit and customer-service performance.

You should also use simulation technology to reduce risk. A simulation model of your business will allow you to eliminate—or at least mitigate—much of the uncertainty that you repeatedly experience when facilitating changes. Gaining a high degree of confidence that your business decisions will succeed is an invaluable benefit of utilizing simulation.

Simulation combines the friendliness of a spreadsheet, the methodology of flow diagramming, the visual benefits of a CAD system, and the intelligence of a facility manager's instincts to help managers make excellent business decisions. It will save you money by helping you avoid inappropriate investments. It will give you confidence in your decisions. When used effectively, it can dramatically improve your bottom line.

▲ Book Overview

To help you develop an appropriate perspective, the first two chapters of this book are presented in the form of short stories. Chapter 1 introduces the concepts of randomness and variability—core ideas upon which simulation technology has been built. Chapter 2 emphasizes the concept of converting an existing "as-is" business environment to a much better "to-be" configuration.

Chapter 3 describes how organizations quantify the value of simulation technology. The focus is on identifying a positive return on investment (ROI) from simulation applications; however, many of the "soft" intangible benefits of the technology (including animation) are also discussed.

Chapter 4 examines the rapid growth in acceptance that the simulation market is experiencing. It features statistics and testimonials that suggest that simulation is emerging as a key technology for corporations around the world. Many quotes and application stories are provided from companies such as Ford, Motorola, Nike, and UPS, along with other testimonials and supporting information from the U.S. government, leading universities, and several international firms.

Simulation's value relative to "neighboring technologies," such as spreadsheets, business diagramming, optimization, and scheduling, is discussed in Chapter 5. These technologies are generally used to solve related problems. This chapter helps clarify the benefits of simulation relative to these tools, and it suggests ways that a simulation strategy can be integrated with them.

Chapter 6 presents a strategy for successfully using simulation technology. It offers advice on when to use simulation, what to do within one's firm before starting a project, and a step-by-step implementation strategy for embracing simulation. The chapter concludes with a recommended strategy for propagating the use of simulation throughout an enterprise.

The final chapter—Chapter 7—suggests what may occur in the future as simulation spreads more aggressively, becoming a mainstream technology that is used by millions of business analysts. Items discussed include market verticalization, real-time system integration, and Internet-enabled applications.

▲ Acknowledgments

Many individuals have helped shape my perspective on this technology—quite a few more than I will mention here. C. Dennis Pegden, CEO/president of Systems Modeling, has had a profound influence on me since he hired me in 1987. Dennis has an uncanny way of simplifying complex subjects to the extent that, after talking with him, I often wonder why I had not figured them out much earlier. He is not only a deep thinker, but an excellent businessman and good friend as well. John Hammann, executive vice president of Systems Modeling and my business mentor of eight years, has helped me translate much of my youthful enthusiasm into a professional perspective. John's unique style and sense of humor have provided great motivation to me over the years. Others at Systems Modeling, such as Deborah Sadowski (the heart and soul of Arena®) and Randy Sadowski, have made unique contributions to my learning process. Lynn Barrett, my primary editor and graphics designer, has also helped tremendously.

Outside of Systems Modeling, I am grateful to many individuals, such as Frank Grange at Perot Systems (whose review of the early drafts of this text was invaluable), Randy Gibson of Automation Associates, Tom McArdle at The SABRE Group, Sue Casey at Visio Corporation, Hwa-Sung Na at Ford Motor Company, Lex Pater at InControl Business Engineers, Michael Drevna at i2 Technologies, Greg Baker at Fluor Daniel, and Barbara Mazziotti at Textile Clothing Technology Corporation, for their help in taking this technology to the level where we all know it belongs—in the mainstream. Any emerging market needs enthusiastic early adopters. This crew has been outstanding in spreading the good news on simulation.

I would also like to recognize several students at the University of Pittsburgh—Andrew Wuertele, Martin Meckesheimer, and Fred Hensel—who built a few simulation models for me early in the process. Their enthusiasm for the book helped me get the project off the ground.

Finally, I want to thank my wife, Linda, for her constant support and critical review of the early drafts of this text. Without her guidance, I would have pursued a number of dead-end streets. I am blessed to have an intelligent partner to keep me moving in a productive direction.

David Profozich

1 Battling a Random World

The power of accurate observation is commonly called cynicism by those who have not got it.

GEORGE BERNARD SHAW

You are a busy executive with a job that pulls you in many directions. You have been working hard for several weeks to prepare a 75-page proposal for a contract that represents the difference between an exceptional year and a mediocre one. Your boss is counting on you to do an outstanding job. Your staff have broken their backs—working evenings and weekends—to help you. And while you are confident that you have done an effective job with the proposal, you intend to use every minute that stands between now (Friday morning) and 5:30 p.m. this afternoon to polish your materials.

The weekend that lies ahead is one that you and your wife have been looking forward to for several months. Two of your best friends—Joe and Chris—are traveling in from the west coast to your Boston home for the weekend. You haven't seen them in years, and you've been daydreaming and chuckling about the fun times you always had together. This weekend is certain to be packed with excellent conversation, delicious food, and some much-needed relaxation.

At 11:30 a.m., your CFO informs you that she is having difficulties creating a cost estimate for a key portion of your proposal. At 1:15 p.m., your boss (the CEO) mentions that he is counting on you to complete the executive summary—a section of the proposal that you were counting on him to create. Your stress level has grown and 5:30 p.m. is coming up quickly.

In spite of the handful of last-minute obstacles (including the fact that your secretary is out sick and you are working with a backup administrative assistant), you are confident that you will successfully complete the proposal on time—and you are beginning to shift some of your focus from today's commitments to tonight's activities.

And then at 1:30 p.m. your phone rings—

... it's your wife, Connie. She tells you that her car won't start, so she can't pick up several key grocery items for tonight's dinner nor will she be able to pick up your three children from school. She has big plans for dinner and desperately needs you to leave the office early to collect the kids, then go shopping, and get home in time so that she can complete the meal. This means you have to walk in the front door with food, beverages, and kids by 6 p.m.—*sharp*.

The level of stress that you were feeling when your boss was in your office earlier today seems insignificant compared to what you are feeling now. In other circumstances, you could tell your wife that you need to finish the proposal before you can even think of leaving. But, considering that you have worked late several nights over the last few weeks, that it's too late to get someone else to pick up your kids, that you promised Connie that last night was the last late night you'd work for a long time, and that it's very important to each of you to be ready for your best friends' arrival, you commit yourself to an extra-special effort.

So you confront a difficult question—*Can you get home on time?*

There is a distinct possibility that you have a very minimal chance of getting everything accomplished by 6 p.m. Unfortunately, on the business front, you aren't aware of any easy solutions that involve off-loading some of your work. And you see no obvious way to unload your personal responsibilities, either. Your family lives in Pittsburgh, so you don't have the convenience of calling a sister or parent to ask for a helping hand.

You sit back in your chair and look at the "to do" list for the proposal. Your heart beats hard. Isn't it amazing how the most difficult times of stress are often those when your business and personal lives get intertwined, and you are struggling to satisfy two of the most influential people in your life—your spouse and your boss. You have two significant missions to accomplish that are extremely time sensitive and very important.

Your immediate concern is that if you do not complete your proposal in a timely manner, you will not leave yourself with a chance to accomplish all of your additional tasks and still get home on time. So, before you can even begin thinking about your journey from the office to your house, you must focus on your office tasks.

You need to get the proposal wrapped up effectively and efficiently so you can get out of your office as quickly as possible. You will need to work hard but be smart—you just can't run out of the office on a $200 million project proposal without finishing strongly. With all that is at stake and after the effort invested, it would be a travesty not to finish the job well.

There are three key proposal tasks that you need to finish—final edits of the proposal body (incorporating your review team's comments), the executive summary, and the final cost estimate. Two of the three do not require the participation of others. Only the final cost estimate requires help—from your CFO.

After you finish these three tasks, you must confer with your administrative assistant to be sure she has all the input she needs so that she can get the proposal out the door on time. She is the one who will take your masterpiece and turn it into professionally bound hard-copy proposals and get them ready for the evening courier pickup.

You know you must complete each task before you can move on to the next. In order to get the job done right, you *estimate* that the following amounts of time are required:

- ▼ Task #1/Final edits—45 minutes
- ▼ Task #2/Executive summary—30 minutes
- ▼ Task #3/Cost estimate—60 minutes
- ▼ Task #4/Prep with assistant—30 minutes

From previous experience, you know that each task may require more or less time than you have estimated. You could make more accurate projections if you had worked on the same project with the same tasks many, many times before. Each time you completed this project, you would record the exact amount of time required for each task. For example, Task #1 (final edits) might have taken you 48, 35, 39, 42, 51, and 42 minutes, respectively, for each of the first six times you performed it. After completing the task many times, you could create a graphical summary of all your final edit times that would look something like Figure 1-1.

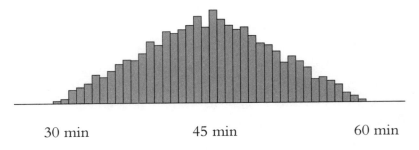

| 30 min | 45 min | 60 min |

Figure 1-1 *Range of Possible Time for Completing Task #1*

Each bar in the chart indicates how often the time value for Task #1 has fallen in a specific time bucket. Examining the pattern, you can say that your most typical time to perform final edits is approximately 45 minutes, consistent with your estimate. Your minimum time is 30 minutes and your maximum is 60 minutes. It is more likely that it will take 45 minutes to get the job done than 55 minutes, but there is a possibility that you will experience a delay that equals any amount of time within the entire range of values.

Since in fact you have not had the luxury of playing out your proposal project hundreds or thousands of times to better understand your expected completion times, you use your life experiences—and "gut feel"—to estimate the amount of time it will take to complete each task.

Taking this approach to Task #2 (executive summary), you estimate it could be complete in 20 minutes, but may—if you experience writer's block—carry out to as much as 50 minutes (after all, this is the centerpiece of your proposal, and doing anything short of an exceptional job would be unacceptable). Your time on Task #3 (cost estimate) poses the largest degree of uncertainty, since you are relying on your CFO to work alongside you. It is possible that this will take as little as 30 minutes, but it could take a whopping 95 minutes. Finally, you will need at least 20 minutes for Task #4 (prep with assistant), and you should be prepared to spend up to 40 minutes before you can safely pack your briefcase and head for your automobile.

The flowchart in Figure 1-2 summarizes the processes (tasks) you must complete before you can begin your journey. Each process is a flowchart component, and for each one, the chart shows the range of possible times that it will take.

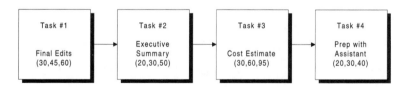

Task #1	Task #2	Task #3	Task #4
Final Edits (30,45,60)	Executive Summary (20,30,50)	Cost Estimate (30,60,95)	Prep with Assistant (20,30,40)

Figure 1-2 *Flowchart of Proposal Effort*

In order to determine when you will wrap up the proposal effort, you could simply add the expected (middle) times of the four processes. The total is $45+30+60+30=165$ minutes, or 2 hours and 45 minutes. It is now 1:30 p.m. If things go as expected, then you will be able to leave your office at 4:15 p.m. However, from previous experience, you know it is unlikely that each task will take the exact amount of time you have estimated. Because of the potential variability, you cannot say with 100% confidence when you will complete the project. The best you can do is estimate your completion time based on experience.

A technology exists, however, that will allow you to examine the situation effectively. This technology allows you to "play out" the tasks to gain an understanding of what you can realistically expect to occur. The only way that you can project with confidence your total proposal completion time is to capture appropriately the processes that you must follow combined with the variability that exists in each one—simulation technology delivers this capability.

By utilizing simulation software, you can create a basic model of any business or personal process in order to understand its behavior over time. In this simple example, you would build a computerized model of your proposal effort. The simulation model will reflect the potential variability in each process. It does so by generating, for each task, a random number within the ranges that you specified when building the model.

For example, one scenario may look like the following:

Final edits—48 minutes
Executive summary—40 minutes
Cost estimate—54 minutes
Prep with administrative assistant—23 minutes

The total time for completion of your proposal in this case is 162 minutes.

A second scenario may look very different. Because of the randomness that is generated by the simulation tool, your time delays for the second "run" of the model may occur like this:

Final edits—60 minutes
Executive summary—28 minutes
Cost estimate—60 minutes
Prep with administrative assistant—28 minutes

In this scenario, your total time is 176 minutes—14 minutes longer than in the first scenario.

Since each scenario that you simulate can have a very different answer, you will need to run the model many times before you can make a confident prediction of your total completion time. I have taken the opportunity to do exactly that. I created a simple simulation model of your proposal effort and executed the model 1,000 times. Here is what I found:

▼ 50% of the time you would be able to leave the office within 165 minutes—by 4:15 p.m.

▼ 75% of the time you would be able to leave the office within 180 minutes—by 4:30 p.m.

▼ 95% of the time you would be able to leave the office within 196 minutes—by 4:46 p.m.

So, thanks to the use of simulation, we now have a much better understanding of what your chances are of getting out the door by 4:15 p.m. Theoretically, your absolute best-case scenario (where every task takes the absolute minimum amount of time) is 100 minutes, and you leave at 3:10 p.m. However, the chance that this would occur is nearly zero. When I ran the model 1,000 times, your best scenario was 128 minutes and a departure at 3:38 p.m. Your worst scenario from the 1,000 runs was 218 minutes and a departure at 5:08 p.m. The likelihood that either extreme scenario would occur is very remote; however, it is often valuable to understand best- and worst-case scenarios when analyzing life situations.

Our effort to predict the total completion time for this very basic four-step process suggests why it is so difficult to deal with variability in your life. Even though we are looking at a very simple step-by-step process, we encounter stress by knowing that the future is unpredictable.

Now, let's turn our attention to the obstacle course awaiting you that takes the form of fighting against traffic, picking up your kids, and shopping before you arrive safely at your home. Here is a step-by-step listing of everything that you must accomplish:

▼ Task #5/Walk to your car

▼ Task #6/Drive to your children's school to pick them up

▼ Task #7/Pick up your children

▼ Task #8/Drive to the market

▼ Task #9/Get money from an automated teller machine (ATM)

▼ Task #10/Shop for all of the groceries that Linda identified in her phone call

▼ Task #11/Drive to your house

In order to determine the total time required to get from your office to your home, we need to expand on the basic analysis that we conducted for the proposal-completion project and again perform a simulation.

First, let's look at the tasks that will take you home:

After you have handed off the proposal to your administrative assistant, you'll have the opportunity to pack your briefcase and walk out the front door of your office building. Your journey home (Task #5) begins with a fast-paced walk to your car. Since you have several intersections to cross, there is some variability in your walk time. Your optimal (lowest) walk time is 5 minutes and your worst case is 9 minutes. Typically, you make it to your car in 7 minutes.

All three of your drive times (Tasks #6, 8, and 11) carry a high degree of potential fluctuation, making it difficult to say exactly how long it will take to get from point *A* to point *B*. The variability comes from a number of sources. Clearly, one source is the number of other drivers on the road and the amount of traffic that may back up at intersections. Other variability may arise from road construction or weather. Your travel speed naturally affects your total drive time (and could even occasion an extended delay to share pleasantries with your local police officer, if you aren't careful). Once again, we confront a number of variables—most of which are out of our control (i.e., traffic, construction, weather). Your minimum, expected, and maximum drive times are listed below:

Task #6—12, 17, 22

Task #8—8, 13, 19

Task #11—18, 23, 31

When you arrive at the school, the first thing you must do is locate your children. Your oldest daughter is usually looking out the classroom window waiting for your arrival. Typically, she can gather your two younger children quickly, so that you have them buckled into their seats in about two minutes (Task #7). At times, however, your children are at the school playground and don't see you arrive. In this case, you have to park and fetch them. The best you can do at school is a quick two-minute turnaround. Your most typical pick-up time is six minutes, and you could get stuck for up to 11 minutes if you have three children who are not cooperating.

Next you are on your way to McTighes outdoor market to pick up the groceries (Task #8). Since you did not expect to shop today, your first stop on arriving at McTighes is at the ATM (Task #9). In the unlikely event that you are the only customer, your total withdrawal time is a mere 45 seconds. Most often there are two people in line—who may be depositing, checking their account balances, and/or withdrawing money. Your expected wait time is two minutes, but it could soar to eight minutes if the line is longer and transactions are numerous.

The biggest unknown of your journey home is the challenge to buy all of the groceries (Task #10). You need to buy crab legs, Italian bread, fresh coffee beans, tomatoes, green beans, and carrot cake at a four-store open-air market. The variability in shopping time that awaits you can be affected by the number of customers who are shopping, the number of clerks helping customers who are selecting or paying for groceries, any difficulty you may have in finding the groceries on your list, and your travel time (walking or jogging) between stores. The fact that you are shopping with your children will not help matters. The best you can hope to do is 11 minutes, and you are certain not to spend more than 29 minutes for your entire shopping experience. Your expected time in the market is 22 minutes.

After you are done shopping, you will begin to get a feel for whether or not you will arrive at your front door on time. At this point, you have successfully dealt with a substantial amount of variability, and you're about to begin the final leg of your journey home (Task #11).

As you begin your drive from the market to your home, your thoughts are drawn to the fun evening before you. If you are keeping pace with the timetable, you are absolutely ecstatic and can spend the remaining few minutes of your drive mentally simulating this evening's events—excellent conversation, a sumptuous meal, a few glasses of wine, and then reminiscing over good times while watching the videotapes you saved from college. However, if you're late, your remaining time in the car is dedicated to planning how you are going to help your wife cook and set the table in time for the 7 p.m. arrival of Joe and Chris.

Now, considering all of the above scenario, what would you say your chances are of making it home by your target time of 6 p.m.? Are you confident in your ability to make it happen? Depending on your level of optimism, your confidence soon may be slightly altered.

When analyzing the simple, four-step process of completing your proposal, we noticed that there was quite a range of possible completion times, because each step carried variability. Now, with seven additional tasks to complete before you make it home, we should expect to find a substantial increase in the overall range of total times.

As we did earlier, if we were simply to add up all of the average or expected times it would take you to perform each process identified in this challenge, your total time would be 255 minutes. In other words, you would walk in the front door of your home at exactly 5:45 p.m. and have plenty of time to help Connie get ready for dinner.

Surely you realize that the probability of having every single event in your obstacle course to success take the expected time is nearly zero. Good judgment tells you that you are bound to experience a good variety of behaviors.

The key here is to recognize that many variables are absolutely beyond your control. In spite of your excellent intentions, enthusiasm for the evening, and strong commitment to making it home on time, you quite simply cannot promise your spouse that you can do it.

In the case of your journey from your office to your home, here's what I found after running the simulation model 1,000 times:

- ▼ 50% of the time you would be able to arrive home within 262 minutes—by 5:52 p.m.
- ▼ 68% of the time you would be able to arrive home within 270 minutes—or 6:00 p.m.
- ▼ 95% of the time you would be able to arrive home within 292 minutes—or 6:22 p.m.

From the 1,000 executions of the simulation model, the worst case was 317 minutes for an arrival time of 6:47 p.m. Although this is very unlikely to occur, at least you would arrive at your home before Joe and Chris. Your best case was 207 minutes for an arrival time of 4:57 p.m. It is too bad you cannot count on enjoying all the extra time after working so hard on the proposal.

The good news is that it appears that you have a good chance to make it home on time. Unfortunately, there is also a reasonable likelihood that you will be slightly late, but not so late that your entire evening is disrupted.

So what is the real lesson we have learned here? It is that randomness and variability surround us. Whether it is the weather, the amount of time it takes you to travel from one location to the next, the time it takes for a letter to reach its destination, the speed of processing your tax return by the IRS, or the outcome of sporting events, we are all faced with an environment that produces results over which we have no control.

However, we are also faced with an environment that applauds one's ability to predict the future. If only we could predict the outcome of our life experiences, we would be in an excellent position to determine when our customers' orders will be finished, when we need to start something in order to finish it on time, and what aspects of our business have the highest impact on our overall performance.

Computer simulation delivers this ability. It is the only technology that truly allows you to forecast the future, taking into consideration all of a system's randomness and variability. In addition to generating values that randomly fall within a specified time range, simulation technology allows you to advance a time clock so that you are able to "fast-forward" to the future. And while a simulation model executes random events over time, it is able to keep track of information for later display. For example, as the model of our project-proposal effort was running, the total completion time was being accumulated for display after the execution.

With simulation, you can confidently say what your performance will be over time—typically within a tight enough range—so that you can make informed decisions regarding your life or business.

In a life situation, your focus might be on the amount of time it takes to get home, complete a project, or read a book. Chances are, you will never apply simulation technology to personal situations, but you certainly could do so if you were able to assess accurately the types of variability within each activity you pursue. In the case of the stressed-out executive, we assumed that we had an excellent ability to estimate accurately the range of possible times, based on our many similar experiences. This helped us create an effective model of our fast-paced journey.

In business, you may be concerned about the total amount of manufacturing time required to assemble or make a product. If you own a delivery company, you are focused on the moment when you can successfully deliver a package to its destination. And if you manage a warehouse, you need to know how much time it will take to retrieve a product, once your customer has ordered it. All of these business examples involve the successful completion of numerous tasks before an ultimate objective is reached—tasks that require varying amounts of time. The only way you can accurately predict your total completion time for all tasks is to use simulation technology to play out the individual events over time.

Randomness—An Additional Perspective

Understanding the effect of randomness and variability on the total amount of time it will take you to perform a series of tasks is one element of concern. Clearly, the business implications of being able to predict completion times are significant. However, we need greater insight into the problems that can be created by randomness.

Take, for example, a very simple single-resource problem. Let us assume that we are examining a simple barber shop. It is very small and has only one chair, as shown in Figure 1-3.

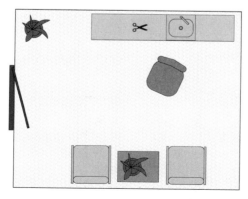

Figure 1-3 The Barber Shop

To illustrate a point, let us first assume that it takes 30 minutes for a barber to service a customer. This includes the actual haircut and the time it takes for the customer to make payment. We will assume that customers arrive exactly on time for their appointments at perfect 30-minute intervals. The barber does not take any breaks. Rather, he continues servicing customers during the entire business day. If we created a small model of this process, we would find that there is absolutely no waiting time for customers. They arrive at the barber shop, immediately sit down in the chair, get a haircut, pay, and leave—passing the next customer on his way to the chair.

Now suppose that the barber shop remains the same and that the barber continues to work without taking any breaks. However, we will introduce randomness to our system in the form of variations in the time between the arrival of customers. Let us assume that our average time of arrival is 30 minutes, but that we experience significant variation in this time.

The simple fact that there is variation in our arrival rate of customers guarantees that the queue inside or in front of the barber shop will continue to grow as long as our shop remains open. For example, at the end of one day, we may have generated a waiting line of six customers. If we could operate the barber shop 24 hours a day for seven straight days and continue to have a steady flow of visitors (averaging one arrival every 30 minutes), we would steadily increase our average number of individuals waiting to get a haircut as time progressed. Theoretically, the customer waiting line would grow to infinity if we let the model run forever. In practical terms, the randomness that exists in our environment creates problems in the form of queues, which may complicate the creation of a plan for any business.

In this example, the only randomness that was introduced was in the arrival rate of customers to the barber shop. It would certainly make sense to add additional variability to our model. If we varied the time required to get a haircut and pay for the service, we would see a more dramatic effect on our customer wait times. Further complication would occur if we allowed the barber to take scheduled and/or random breaks.

This example explains why businesses such as barber shops, exclusive restaurants, and doctors must take appointments. Without incorporating some control over the way incoming patients or customers behave, it would be impossible to avoid extremely long wait times due to the variability that occurs in individuals' behavior. Taking the randomness out of the system allows businesses to function smoothly.

Unfortunately, most business enterprises in the world today do not have the luxury of taking randomness out of the business equation. Variability surrounds the business enterprise in many different forms. The ideas of randomness and variability are clearly central to an understanding of computer simulation. Simulation technology gives you the opportunity to understand realistically the effects of randomness and variability on your business. But randomness and variability only scratch the surface in characterizing the central ideas of this powerful technology. Read on.

2   Moving from "As-Is" to "To-Be"

Failure is the opportunity to begin again more intelligently.

HENRY FORD

In Chapter 1 we were concerned with the many variables that lay between the moment when you got the phone call from your wife and the moment when you walked through your front door. As a stressed executive encountering these variables on your way home, you were an individual navigating a system. The system that you navigated (i.e., the proposal effort, the roads, the outdoor market) was fixed. You had no control over the system configuration. Unfortunately, you did not even have control over the time of day when you started your journey.

Now, let's take a small portion of your entire odyssey and analyze it more carefully. In this chapter, you are no longer the troubled executive who is charging to arrive home on time. Instead, you are the owner of McTighes market. The challenge before you is to gain a better understanding of what happens within your market—to your customers—so that you are in a better position to make improvements. In this case, you have total control over the system and very little control over the individuals who are moving through it.

You are aware of the fact that your customers are not satisfied with your service times. They and your employees have informed you that you are beginning to lose business to the large grocery store across the river. While your customers generally prefer your products, their unwillingness to spend the extra time waiting in line to make purchases is beginning to turn them away. You are reluctant to increase the cost of operating your business by adding to or changing your staff schedule, but you know that you must do something quickly or else lose valuable customers and essential profits.

Based on your business experience, you are confident that you can win back your lost customers—and even attract newcomers—if you improve customer-service levels to make McTighes market a more attractive place to shop. You decide that you must decrease the amount of time that your customers wait in line to two minutes or less at each store.

The key question you must answer is: *"What is my best staffing strategy to ensure that my customers are serviced quickly?"*

You will need to know how many staff members, and what specific staffing schedule, are necessary to achieve your customer-service objectives. You may also need to consider adding service-counter space, but you believe that a more effective staffing policy will make this unnecessary.

You could try to solve your problem by trial and error. You could try varying staff strategies until you are satisfied with the results. It might take you several weeks or more, and you might end up hiring (and training) more staff than necessary, but you could eventually improve your system in this manner.

Lucky for you, however, you have a niece—Valerie—who has encountered simulation technology in her business curriculum at Boston College. She is on semester break and has offered to help you deal with your situation more effectively. Valerie offers to build a simple simulation model of your market in order to help you improve your customer-service levels. Fortunately, Valerie is a dynamic young lady, and she is able to draft a few of her friends to help collect information from your market for the simulation study.

Valerie starts out by analyzing the existing market. It consists of four stores and has a very basic configuration, as shown in Figure 2-1:

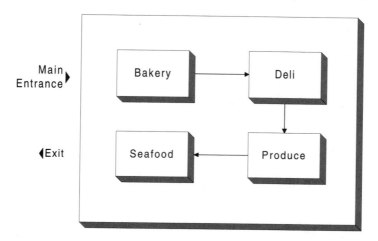

Figure 2-1 *McTighes Market*

Customers always arrive at the main entrance, which is located at the bakery. Because of the layout of the market, they always visit the bakery, deli, produce, and seafood stores in this order. Every customer, however, does not necessarily shop at every store. Any customer may shop at one, two, three, or all four stores during a single visit to McTighes. Customers' decisions to shop at certain stores are affected by the time of day and type of products offered. For example, customers tend not to buy much seafood at 8 in the morning, and sales at the bakery slow considerably during the late afternoon.

In Chapter 1, we were not concerned with the specifics of what occurred when a customer (the stressed executive) entered the market. We simply considered the total amount of shopping time as a single variable. Now, however, we must recognize that customers exhibit a significant amount of variability in their behavior within your market. The number of stores that they patronize will vary from customer to customer and from visit to visit. Once inside a store, their shopping time can vary substantially depending upon the size of their grocery list, the amount of congestion, and various anomalies such as stopping to chat with a friend. The individual possibilities are many, but Valerie is able to collect specific items of information in order to analyze this system.

For simplicity's sake, we'll assume that each store has an identical layout, as shown in Figure 2-2.

The layout consists of a large service counter where your staff is working. Most of the products that you sell are requested by your customers and your staff retrieves them, although you do have a few products (such as cocktail sauce in the seafood store) that customers can retrieve on their own. Your customers wait in line to be served by one of your staff. Once a customer order (which can vary in terms of the number of products requested) has been satisfied, the person who is helping the customer takes payment for the groceries, places them in a bag, and moves on to the next customer.

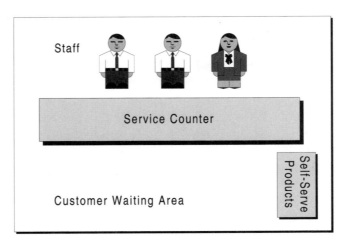

Figure 2-2 *Layout of Store*

The service counter in each store has capacity for three individuals to be working simultaneously; however, you do not always have all three workers on the clock. Rather, you have a staff schedule in each store that varies with the time of day. For example, you typically have only a single worker in the seafood store early in the morning since most customers do not shop there until after 10 a.m. You have identified three basic shifts that break up each day into distinct sections. Your staff schedule matches these three distinct times of the day. The morning shift begins at 6 a.m. and ends at 10 a.m. The midday shift starts at 10 a.m. and wraps up at 2 p.m. Your final shift starts at 2 p.m. and ends at 6 p.m. (See Table 2-1.) All of your stores close at 6 p.m.

Table 2-1 *Schedule for Three Shifts*

	Shift Starts	Shift Ends
Morning	6 a.m.	10 a.m.
Midday	10 a.m.	2 p.m.
Afternoon	2 p.m.	6 p.m.

In order to build a simulation model of your market, Valerie will need to study your customers' behaviors for a period of two weeks. She recognizes that the more information she can collect, the better her simulation model will be, but she feels that two weeks of market activity will serve as an adequate sample of how your customers behave.

Valerie and her friends will need to identify the following information:

▼ Total number of customers entering your market per shift

▼ Number of customers entering each store per shift

▼ Number of products purchased at each store per customer

▼ Customer-service times (how long it takes for your staff to service a customer)

▼ Current staff schedule for each store

▼ Amount of time required to walk from store to store

In the previous chapter, we recognized that there was no realistic way for us to repeat the same proposal effort hundreds or thousands of times in order to record the actual completion times for final edits, the executive summary, and so on. Instead, we relied upon intelligent estimates for our minimum, expected, and maximum time values for each process. For this example, however, Valerie has the luxury of being able to study the activities in your market to represent accurately in the simulation model the true behaviors of your customers and staff. By basing the model on actual recorded behaviors, Valerie will be able to create a simulation that is much more reliable than one created on the basis of "gut-feel" information.

Valerie also recognizes that there is substantial variability in the time intervals between the arrival of customers to your market, the number of products purchased in each store, customer-service times, and walk times between stores. She will represent these types of information in the form of random distributions, as we did in Chapter 1. She will accomplish this by taking all of the individual behaviors of your customers over the two-week period and converting them into an appropriate distribution, so that the simulation-software product will be able to predict the future with an accurate assessment of the variability in your customers' shopping habits. Valerie can convert the customer data directly to a distribution by using software tools designed for this purpose.

Other information, such as the number of individuals working on the current staff schedule, does not vary dynamically. During each shift, there is a known number of staff. Staff size may vary during the shift changes, but it remains constant during a single shift. The simulation model of McTighes market will be created with the assumption that the staff schedule remains steady throughout a single shift.

▣ Collecting Data

Valerie's first task is to collect information. She and her friends will record the behaviors of your customers and the amounts of time that it takes for your staff to service customers. The members of Valerie's simulation team will be assigned to your stores and will use a palmtop computer in order to record quickly the activities that occur in your market. Valerie's friends will also work outdoors for a period of time recording the walking times of customers as they move from one store to the next.

After compiling the data, here is what Valerie and her friends learned about your market:

▼ 7,534 customers visited McTighes market over a two-week period

- ◆ 1,680 during the morning shift
- ◆ 3,366 during the midday shift
- ◆ 2,488 during the late afternoon/dinner shift

▼ During the morning shift:

- ◆ 85% (or 1,428) customers visited the bakery
- ◆ 18% (or 302) visited the deli
- ◆ 15% (or 252) shopped at the produce store
- ◆ 1% (or 17) shopped at the seafood store

Similar information was collected for each of the other two shifts. For the midday shift, 45% of your customers visited the bakery; 58%, the deli; 44%, produce; and 28%, seafood. During the late afternoon, your breakdown of visitors was 15%, 62%, 55%, and 30%, respectively.

To capture appropriately the variability that exists in the number of products purchased by customers, the customer-service times, and the customer walking times, Valerie and her friends recorded the individual events that occurred in each case. For example, they amassed a data file for each store that looks something like Table 2-2. Each value in the table represents the unique experience of a single customer who shopped at the deli.

Table 2-2 Data File from Deli

Customer	# of Items	Service Time
1	5	2.4
2	8	3.8
3	4	1.8
4	12	5.6
5	3	1.3
6	8	3.7
7	14	6.3

By recording the behaviors of each customer who shopped in McTighes market, Valerie and her friends were able to create a large sample of observations. This large sample helps to ensure that the true system variability that exists in the market is adequately represented in the simulation model.

Once all of the market data had been collected, it was time to generate appropriate distributions for the model.

▲ Depicting Randomness

For each time delay in the previous chapter, we assumed that a minimum, expected, and maximum value existed. To describe this information within a simulation model, we used a distribution of times that looked something like Figure 2-3.

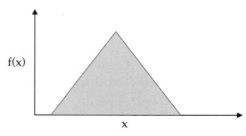

Figure 2-3 Example Distribution #1

You will notice that there is a well-balanced range of acceptable values between our minimum and maximum values and that the most typically occurring values fall near the center of the range.

In other circumstances, the observations we record from a system to be modeled may not be so conveniently balanced. They may look something like Figure 2-4. Here, many more observations have small values than have large values.

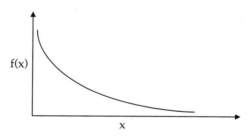

Figure 2-4 *Example Distribution #2*

The key is to collect all of the information about how a process behaves and determine the best way to describe it within a simulation model. Software programs that automatically convert your data to statistical distributions will do this work for you. Distributions such as triangular, exponential, uniform, and normal are used by simulation software to generate random numbers. Each distribution mimics random behavior in a different way. Since each distribution can differ significantly, it is important to make certain that the information you are analyzing is represented with the appropriate distribution.

In the case of the morning shift at the bakery, Valerie would take the 1,428 observations recorded and read all of them directly into the software program, which would generate the distribution that best depicts the dynamic nature of customers' shopping habits. In this case, the focus is on the number of products purchased. From all of the observations, the following distribution is generated:

Triangular(2, 4, 8)

33

This distribution means that the minimum number of items purchased by your customers is two, the most typically occurring is four, and the maximum is eight.

Valerie could use a single model to capture your market's behavior for all three shifts. In this case, however, she decides to analyze each shift independently. She will make a staffing recommendation that is unique for each significant time period. For this example, we will focus specifically on the morning shift.

After Valerie and her friends have gathered all of the appropriate information on the morning shift in your market, they will generate the following distributions to characterize the key dynamic activities:

Arrival rate of customers to your market. Based on her team's review of your customer behavior, Valerie recognizes that approximately 30 customers arrive at your market per hour, or approximately one customer every two minutes. Customers, however, do not arrive at perfect two-minute intervals—rather, they arrive according to a random distribution. Valerie understands that most customer-arrival patterns in business applications of this kind are modeled by using the exponential distribution where only an average is specified. As a result, she uses the following distribution to describe customer arrivals to the market:

Exponential(2)

Number of items purchased. Here, a unique set of observations will be obtained for each of the four stores. We have already discussed the bakery (which was characterized by using a triangular distribution). In the deli, people tend to buy more items per person than they do in the bakery. This tendency was reflected in the information collected. The distributions shown in Table 2-3—all triangular—were generated to characterize the number of items purchased by store.

Table 2-3 Number of Goods Purchased

Number of Goods Purchased per Customer	
Bakery	Triangular(2, 4, 8)
Deli	Triangular(2, 8, 16)
Produce	Triangular(1, 2, 3)
Seafood	Triangular(1, 1, 3)

Each value is represented in the form of a distribution of times. In the seafood market, most customers buy a single product, which explains why the minimum and most typically occurring values are both 1. Although Valerie does not have a statistics background, she is confident that she has identified the right distributions for this model, since she and her friends collected ample information and then used an appropriate distribution–fitting software product.

Customer-service level. When they moved from one store to the next, Valerie and her friends identified some differences in the amount of time it took for your staff to service customers. For example, the average time that your staff took to slice lunch meat, bag it, and hand it to your customers was about 45 seconds per item. To determine the amount of time *per item* required to service customers, Valerie took the total service time of each customer and divided it by the number of items they purchased. She then used all of these values to determine the customer-service levels stated in Table 2-4.

Table 2-4 Service Times

Service Times per Item	
Bakery	Normal(30 seconds, 5 seconds)
Deli	Normal(45 seconds, 6 seconds)
Produce	Normal(27 seconds, 5 seconds)
Seafood	Normal(27 seconds, 5 seconds)

In the case of service times, normal distributions were used where an average time is specified along with an amount of variation from the average (known as a standard deviation). In the case of the bakery service times, Table 2-4 states that on average it takes 30 seconds to offer one product to a customer and that most of the total observations are within five seconds of this value. Again, this is simply an additional way to represent the variability that takes place in our market.

Customer walk times. There is not a tremendous amount of variability in your customer walk times as they move between stores. If she wanted to, Valerie could have ignored this variability and could still have predicted the system behavior with a high degree of accuracy. But because your niece is a perfectionist, she decided to go through the same procedure for walk time as she did for the other dynamic system components. Valerie found that your customers average a one-minute walk between stores and that most of the walk times are between 45 and 75 seconds. As a result, she uses the following distribution for walk times:

Normal(60 seconds, 15 seconds)

■ Simulating the Market

Once all of the necessary market data has been captured and converted to distributions (where necessary), the simulation model can be constructed quickly. Valerie no longer requires the help of her friends; she can easily wrap up the project on her own.

The first step in creating the model will be to build a logical flow diagram of your business—similar to the one in Chapter 1. Building a flow diagram of the processes that take place in your market is easy. The diagram identifies the specific events that occur as a customer shops in your stores, as shown in Figure 2-5.

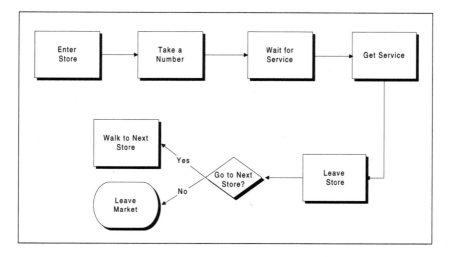

Figure 2-5 *Flow of Customer Processes in Each Store*

This diagram is repeated for each store that a customer visits. As you can see, after shopping at one store, the customer may or may not go to another one in your market. This decision will be based on probabilities consistent with what we learned earlier about your customers' behaviors. For example, there is a 35% chance that a customer will shop at the deli during the morning shift. Obviously, then, 65% of your customers will not.

The flow diagram in this chapter is slightly different from the one in Chapter 1. There, as the executive, you followed a serial process (one after the next) in order to get the proposal and other activities done. In this case, however, we encounter a situation where a selection must be made from two alternatives. There is a chance at each transition point that a customer will either go to an additional store or leave the market entirely. Many life situations are this way. As we navigate from one experience to the next, we are often faced with alternatives that can dramatically affect the outcome of our day. Although we all deal with certain responsibilities in life that require consistent behavior—such as a specific appointment to meet with a customer or the need to file a tax report on time—many other experiences do not occur in a predictable "one-after-the-next" format. The same holds true in business or in our market example.

Now it is time for Valerie to create a simulation model of your market and make the best recommendation she possibly can. From a completed flow diagram, she can very easily construct a simulation model of the market (in fact, with some simulation-software tools, this can be done automatically).

The flow diagram effectively charts the process steps that individual customers follow when shopping in each of your stores. However, it ignores one significant issue: it does not consider your staff schedule. The staff schedule will naturally affect the amount of time customers will wait to be serviced.

Your existing staff schedule for the morning shift is: Bakery—2 workers; Deli—2 workers; Produce—1 worker; Seafood—1 worker.

▪ Establishing the "As-Is" Model

With the simulation model complete, Valerie will now execute the model to understand how your customer-service times will fare. Remember, we are starting by simulating the existing market conditions, so you should expect the initial model to replay the performance that you have come to expect (and be frustrated by). We call it an "as-is" model, since it is meant to capture the behaviors of the current environment.

The "as-is" simulation model serves several purposes. First, it allows us to make certain that the model accurately captures the intricacies of our system's behavior. It is very important to make certain that the actual system performance is replayed within the simulation model. In fact, if actual historical information is entered into the model—rather than variable data—the output of the model should be precisely consistent with what occurred in the real world.

Generating an "as–is" simulation model that perfectly mimics a real system also adds instant credibility to the project and gives us the confidence to take a step forward toward determining the ultimate "to–be" system configuration. Getting from "as–is" to "to–be" in our market example may not be terribly difficult, although, in many systems an extremely large number of configuration possibilities may stand between the two.

In addition to serving as a launch point for conducting "what-if" analysis, the "as–is" model serves as a baseline against which to compare performance of the many candidate "to–be" configurations. The number of "to–be" alternative configurations depends on the analysts' abilities to hypothesize alternative scenarios and an organization's patience in waiting for comprehensive experimentation to take place. Figure 2-6 depicts the process of moving from "as–is" to "to–be."

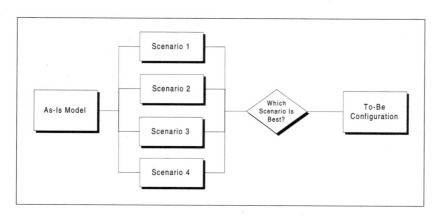

Figure 2-6 "What-If" Analysis: Getting from "As-Is" to "To-Be"

Often within a very short time frame you will be able to identify a "to–be" system configuration that is acceptable. If you are dealing with a situation where there are many possible scenarios, the question ultimately becomes, "Is it worth working to try to find a better solution, or is it time to move forward with an implementation strategy?" While some simulation-software tools offer features that make the process of identifying alternatives easier than others, it is the simulation analyst who will eventually make the call on how much "what-if" analysis is appropriate before a "to-be" scenario is selected.

Now, if our primary objective in managing our market was to gain a better understanding of how long customers wait in line today, we would not need to build a simulation model of our business. Rather, we could simply have our time-counting staff record customer wait times and the total amount of time that your cashiers served customers. However, since we are working to upgrade your existing business performance, we need to first construct a model of an "as-is" configuration before we can take the next step.

To answer the question from the beginning of this chapter— *What is my best staffing strategy to ensure that my customers are serviced quickly (do not have to spend more than two minutes per store waiting in lines)?*—we need to try different staffing configurations in order to determine the most cost-effective way to improve customer-service times.

You might assume that the solution will be to increase your staffing commitment. But rather than simply hiring new employees, we can first try to use simulation technology to help us identify any possibilities that may exist for improving system performance with your present resources. If we cannot find a good way to manage your business with the current staff configuration, we will begin exploring alternatives that require increased investment. Ultimately, we will be able to determine the right staffing configuration to get the job done without wasting money on unnecessary workers.

Let's briefly examine the performance of the "as-is" market configuration. Valerie's model does, in fact, capture the flawed system of today.

From the output summary in Table 2-5, we see that the customer wait times at the bakery average 2.8 minutes. This is consistent with your current system, and you find this performance to be unacceptable. Your customer-service times at the deli are tolerable, and the service times at produce and seafood are extremely low. Valerie also notes that your staff in the deli are busy only 49% of the time compared to an 80% utilization in the bakery.

Table 2-5 *"As-Is" Model Output*

	# of Clerks	Avg. Wait (min.)	Max. Wait (min.)	Avg. Queue Length	Max. Queue Length	Util. of Staff
			"As-Is" Market			
Bakery	2	2.8	28	2.02	25	80%
Deli	2	1.1	25	0.17	9	49%
Produce	1	0.03	2	0.0	2	9%
Seafood	1	0.0	0	0.0	0	0%

To develop a solid understanding of our expected total time for completing all of our tasks in Chapter 1, we executed the simulation hundreds of times. This allowed us to create many, many scenarios so that we could then assess what was likely to occur. In the market example, however, we can run our model once—for many, many days of operation—to understand the system. This is because the customers within the market exhibit significant variability. Since hundreds of customers move through your market each day, we are certain to generate enough activities to get a good feel for how the market will perform.

■ Identifying the "To-Be" Scenario

Valerie is satisfied that she has successfully modeled your "as-is" market. Since her simulation model accurately recreated the flawed performance of your current market, she is ready to move on to evaluating additional scenarios, so that she can determine the ultimate "to-be" configuration that you and your customers seek.

She proceeds in her study by trying different hypothetical staffing scenarios. The baseline "as-is" model does not change. Customers continue to exhibit the same shopping behaviors that they did previously. Only the staff schedule changes.

As you can imagine, there are many possible staffing configurations. If you had unlimited time and patience, you could try every single imaginable scenario for staffing your market. If you did, you would generate a staff schedule that was optimized according to your objective (in this case, for the lowest customer-service times). However, in the real world, you can typically establish a dramatically improved system performance by trying out a reasonable number of feasible solutions and picking the one that gives you the best performance.

The first scenario Valerie tries is to move one of your staff from the deli to the bakery, since there is a higher percentage of customers at the bakery and since your staff in the deli appear to be underutilized. She figures that this may provide a better balance to your customer-service times. Unfortunately, as you can see in Table 2-6, the customer wait times in the deli skyrocket to such a high level that your overall market performance would be worse.

Customers average 103 minutes of wait time in the deli when only one clerk is working to service them. At worst case, a 253-minute wait is incurred. This is hardly a move in favor of satisfying your customers.

Table 2-6 *Scenario 1 Model Output*

| | Scenario 1 | | | | | |
	# of Clerks	Avg. Wait (min.)	Max. Wait (min.)	Avg. Queue Length	Max. Queue Length	Util. of Staff
Bakery	3	0.31	8	0.22	13	53%
Deli	1	103	253	151	41	98%
Produce	1	0.03	2	0	2	9%
Seafood	1	0	0	0	0	0%

Knowing that Scenario 1 is unacceptable, Valerie continues her analysis. She tries something you may never have considered. She staffs your bakery with three workers, leaves two at the deli, and one at produce, and chooses not to staff the seafood store. After running the model, you find that your customer-service times across all three stores are outstanding, as shown in Table 2-7. You will clearly have very satisfied customers.

Valerie has identified a scenario that makes your greatest average wait time a mere 1.1 minutes. This is exactly what you had hoped for, and you know that it would help you alleviate the problem that brought you to this project in the first place. The only problem with this scenario is that you no longer have staff at the seafood store.

Table 2-7 Scenario 2 Model Output

	# of Clerks	Avg. Wait (min.)	Max. Wait (min.)	Avg. Queue Length	Max. Queue Length	Util. of Staff
			Scenario 2			
Bakery	3	0.31	8	0.22	13	53%
Deli	2	1.1	19	0.17	6	49%
Produce	1	0.03	2	0.0	2	9%
Seafood	none	none	none	none	none	none

You might ask yourself whether you need to have the seafood store open during the morning shift. You might decide to open it at 10 a.m. rather than 6 a.m., since you average only two customers per day in this time slot. Another option is to add one person to your staffing mix so that you have coverage in all four stores for the morning. Of course, this costs you money, but you should have expected that you might need to spend more to improve your customer-service levels.

By using a simulation model, Valerie was able to find a system configuration that did not increase your costs and that may be acceptable. You must ultimately decide whether it is acceptable to close the seafood store for the morning shift.

In addition to projecting our total customer-service times, our simulation model allowed us to determine how busy our clerks were during the run. The percentage of time that they helped customers was generated by the model. This staff-utilization data helped us to understand whether we had an appropriate staffing strategy. In this example, we were not as concerned with your staff-utilization percentages as we were with your customer-service performance. However, in other circumstances, you may want to look closely at staff-utilization levels to see if you are over- or underutilizing your key workers. You may be able to shift individuals who aren't very busy into more productive roles in another store.

Suppose you decide to add one staff to your market, and it costs you $13,000 per year. You calculate that you have been losing 2% of your customers per month with the customer service at the previous level—which costs you approximately $100,000 per year in profit. So by adding a single staff member, you are deciding to spend $13,000 per year to avoid losing $100,000 in one year. You are also avoiding other ill effects of offering poor customer service, such as the lack of customer referrals. Ultimately, too, you are avoiding an even greater loss in profit, which would occur as your bad reputation spread.

In this simple example, clearly you generate a very positive return on your investment in added staff. It is easy to apply this example to many business problems in manufacturing or service industries. In manufacturing, the stores are machines, the space between stores may be aisles or conveyors, orders may require a varying number of component parts (versus the items on the shopping list), and service times may represent inventory waiting to be converted to finished goods.

In a service application—say a call-center environment at a credit-card company, where operators are helping customers—the stores are operators, the people are customer calls coming into the center, and, rather than waiting to buy groceries, callers wait on hold to be serviced by an operator.

The key point in this chapter is that simulation technology provides a very powerful way to move from an "as-is" system to an ultimate "to-be" system. It does so by accurately capturing the behavior of the original system and then hypothetically changing the system until the best scenario is identified. By conducting "what-if" analysis, the simulation analyst should be able to find a far better solution to a business application than could have been determined without the technology.

▪ Central Concepts Summarized

Before moving on, I would like to summarize a few key realities in business that have created the need for broad usage of simulation technology:

▼ Variability can have a major influence on system performance. A system that works fine with constant processes may perform poorly with variability in the processes. If, when conducting analysis, you don't adequately capture system variability, you'll have a distorted view of the system's performance.

▼ You cannot use a static tool to study a dynamic problem. A static tool gives an optimistic performance assessment. The greater the variability in the system, the greater the error in static analysis. (See Chapters 3 and 5 for further discussion.)

▼ There are three basic ways to improve a system's performance:

♦ Add resources (e.g., operators, machines) while keeping the process and variability the same.

♦ Reduce variability. This may be done by scheduling appointments or other specific events. In some applications, variability may be reduced by having backup systems or by adding preventive maintenance in order to reduce the risk of failed resources.

♦ Reengineer the process.

Simulation technology allows you to capture system variability adequately so that you can effectively explore various alternatives for improving system performance. In Chapter 3, we will focus on ways in which you can utilize simulation technology within your organization to achieve a positive return on investment (ROI).

The Value of Simulation

Leadership is about taking an organization to a place it would not have otherwise gone without you, in a value-adding, measurable way.

GEORGE M. C. FISHER

Understanding the impact of randomness and variability in a business environment is extremely valuable. Being able to predict the future accurately is very useful. Gaining the luxury of playing hypothetical "what-if" scenarios on a computer model without disturbing an actual system also can make a significant impact on strategic decisions. Why then do some organizations struggle when it comes to accepting simulation as a key component of their business-strategy toolbox?

One answer is that today's business managers often are unaware of the value that simulation adds to their business. They have not had firsthand experience with the technology. Although simulation technology has existed in some form for several decades, it has largely been confined inside corporate research laboratories or very specialized engineering departments and has not received the enterprisewide visibility that it deserves.

Until recently, too, the use of simulation-software technology was a significant programming challenge. The level of effort required to implement simulation was too steep—requiring computer-savvy "black belts" to apply it successfully—and the computer hardware required to execute models successfully was too costly. This problem has diminished in the 1990s with the advances made by the simulation-software industry and with the dramatic price/performance improvements by the PC industry. Software products are now available that share the development architecture of Microsoft® software, a Windows® operating system orientation, a flow-diagram model development strategy and that can be implemented with relative ease on 486- or Pentium-based personal computers.

Another hindrance is that some companies are presently using other technologies, such as spreadsheets and other planning systems, to make strategic decisions. They believe that they are getting "acceptable" solutions and are unaware that they could be making far better decisions based on simulation applications.

For simulation to make an impact in your company, you need to understand—and believe in—the value that simulation can add. By gaining an awareness of how to quantify the value of simulation routinely, you will become more effective at managing the implementation of the tool to its best effect within your company.

This chapter is dedicated to identifying the value that simulation technology offers to improve business performance. By the time you complete it, you will be able to state concisely why this technology is meaningful for effective business engineering. You will also learn many of the softer benefits of using simulation technology. These other benefits—although they are difficult to assess in terms of specific bottom-line impact—are also very important to consider.

◼ Two Approaches for Quantifying Value

By identifying the best "to-be" business model that can possibly be defined, companies can get the maximum performance from their resources and achieve dramatic financial benefits. Simulation technology can save you money by helping you avoid unnecessary expenditures. It can save you money by reducing your investment in maintaining inventory. It can save you money by helping you optimize the layout of your business. The key is to know when to use this technology to make your business more effective and how to keep score of your success along the way.

The approach for stating a specific return on investment (ROI) derived from a simulation study varies, depending on whether an existing "as–is" system can be used as a benchmark for evaluating proposed "to–be" scenarios. If you are moving from an "as–is" to a "to–be" configuration, you should easily be able to cite specific improvements and related dollar savings. In this case, it should not be difficult to assess your existing cost, profit, and customer-service levels so that you can compare each "to–be" scenario against your original performance. Stating an ROI often becomes an effort of basic mathematics.

On the other hand, stating an ROI when using simulation to design a new system is a bit more challenging. Of course, you can always compare each candidate "to–be" business scenario against the others and specifically show how the cost-for-performance of one scenario exceeds that of another (or all others) by a certain amount. This may be enough to satisfy you and your management. However, you do not in this case have the luxury of an "as–is" system against which to benchmark your "to–be" alternatives.

Because the amount of cost savings to be realized is important, I encourage you to cite an ROI when designing new systems—even though you may lack an "as–is" benchmark. To do so, you will need to identify what the recommended solution to the business problem would have been if you had not used simulation to facilitate the design. Chances are that your company previously used an alternative planning methodology against which you can compare the results of your simulation effort. This comparison will help you gain greater insight into the value of simulation, and it will help your company become more aware of its potential across the enterprise.

▮ The Value of Simulation Quantified

As business professionals, we should all aspire to leverage information technology to make us more productive and allow us to save more money than we spend. Some basic desktop tools—such as word processors and electronic-mail systems—are valued highly because they make us more effective at managing our daily business functions. Simulation, however, not only makes analysts more productive—it often generates results that can be expressed in terms of a compelling ROI. Let's take a look at how the value can be quantified.

▲ Resource Planning

As Peter Drucker, the great management visionary of the mid-20th century, stated concisely, "Productivity means that balance between all factors of production that will give the greatest output for the smallest effort." At the most fundamental level, businesses today need to get the maximum output from their limited resources. The specific ratio of inputs to outputs is referred to as the *efficiency* of a system. When designing a new facility or considering a change to an existing business, we must plan to ensure the most effective use of available resources. Resources in business are people, machines, motor vehicles, computer equipment, floor space, and any other instrument used to convert inputs to outputs. The performance that you desire may be defined as efficient manufacturing of a product, successful creation of a computer program, or timely servicing of a customer problem. The challenge is to decide on a portfolio of resources and put them to work in your business so that you come as close as humanly possible to optimizing your business performance.

Simulation technology is often used to facilitate resource-capacity investment decisions. The ultimate goal is to invest in the "right" amount of capacity to manage your business effectively. The quantified value of conducting a simulation study is often expressed as a specific savings that was derived because the model helped an organization purchase less capacity than it previously did or normally would. In order to understand the effect of any proposed configuration of critical resources, you need to play out the system's behavior in a dynamic fashion. By playing out many different capacity scenarios, you should be able to select the implementation strategy that is most cost effective.

Your objective is to achieve your throughput and service-level targets without overspending for capacity. Just as in our McTighes-market example, you want to purchase enough capacity to get the job done effectively without wasting money on unnecessary excess capacity.

Planning for an appropriate or optimal amount of capacity can be a challenge. To explore this idea, let us assume that you are a manager of a manufacturing facility. Your plant makes small engines that are used in outdoor gardening equipment. You happen to be working for a progressive company that is constantly upgrading plants in order to leverage the latest manufacturing technology. Within the past few years, you have watched your operation move from a low technology, largely manual operation to a mixed manual and auto-mated environment with the latest machinery.

Each time you upgrade your facility, you must purchase new machines for producing your products. They cost approximately $300,000 each. You have a good forecast from sales indicating what the total manufacturing output of your plant needs to be for the coming three years. You have been told by your boss (a senior vice president) that you must never have a situation where orders cannot be processed on time due to a lack of machine capacity. Fortunately, you will not run out of raw materials to feed your system.

The process or flow through which your products travel is fairly easy to flowchart and contains some variability and randomness. The variability stems from failures in your equipment, scheduled main-tenance, and fluctuations in manufacturing process rates. It is very difficult for you to determine an appropriate number of machines to purchase for your plant upgrade without conducting an appro-priate simulation analysis.

We will quantify the value of simulation in this example as follows. First we will use the tool to determine the "right" or optimal number of machines for your plant. We will do so by building a model and conducting tests on a number of system configurations, each involving a different number of machines. We will execute our manufacturing orders through each configuration in order to compare the performance of one against the next.

The findings of our simulation-based research for one month of production may look something like Table 3-1. Here, with the addition of each machine, we improve our ability to deliver a greater percentage of products on time. However, we also increase our costs in doing so. Another significant issue is the percentage of time that the machines would be busy. Suppose, for example, that the equipment you are using has a recommended maximum utilization of 87%. You realize that you should not exceed this limit, or you will become vulnerable to high service charges.

Table 3-1 Production Research Results

# of Machines	% of Products Completed on Time	Machine Utilization
3	55%	.98
4	63%	.97
5	73%	.97
6	81%	.97
7	86%	.95
8	90%	.93
9	93%	.89
10	96%	.86
11	99%	.85

You may determine that 10 machines is the best configuration for the system, because it allows you to achieve your vice president's target performance. Buying an 11th machine would cost at least an additional $300,000 and is not necessary. So you walk into your vice president's office and strongly recommend the purchase of 10 machines. You also proudly report that you are confident you have saved your organization a significant amount of money by using simulation. Your vice president seems enthusiastic, but she asks you to tell her *how much* you have saved.

To quantify the value of simulation in this application, you must prove that your simulation-based decision is better than the decision you would have made if you had used a traditional nondynamic methodology in order to determine capacity requirements for plant changes. Fortunately, you are able to do this.

The methodology that you would have used consists of spreadsheets containing mathematical equations that do not incorporate randomness, variability, or the concept of a moving time clock. You would not have captured the dynamics of your system, placing you at a high risk in making an investment decision on the number of machines to purchase. (A further discussion of spreadsheet-based analysis is given in Chapter 5.)

By using the mathematically based system, you would have found yourself rounding up (i.e., buying more equipment than the spreadsheet indicated) in order to increase your chances of getting the desired output from your plant. Unfortunately, however, you were underutilizing your equipment and overspending. If you had used the traditional method of determining the number of required machines, you would have recommended 13 machines as a "safe" investment to get the job done. In this case, you would have purchased an additional $900,000 in equipment and would not have significantly affected your system's performance. Simulation technology helped you, in this case, achieve a cost savings of $900,000.

If we assume that the amount of money you invested in the simulation study—analysis time, software, computer equipment, etc.—totaled $50,000, you can document an immediate ROI of *1,800%*! Beyond this, you now have a model of your new system configuration that can be used when making the next major facility change.

Savings realized in the form of avoided capital purchases are one way to quantify the value of simulation. This value-determining strategy works well if you are migrating from a nondynamic to a simulation-based methodology for sizing your capacity needs, where you can compare the recommendations of each system and quantify the savings.

Another way to use the simulation model to quantify a return would be to evaluate the improvements in total system performance by adding incremental resources. For example, if two additional machines at $300,000 each increase your ability to respond to customers by 30% and consequently allow you to ship more orders and dramatically improve customer service, you may be able to recognize a dramatic ROI by exploring this scenario. Without being able to play out the behavior of this system in a simulation model, you might not be able to understand the impact of this possibility accurately.

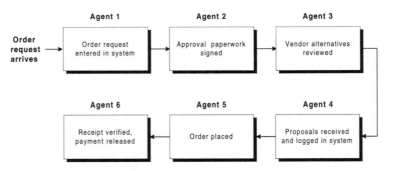

Figure 3-1 *Flow Diagram of "As-Is" Purchasing Configuration*

Often, you can eliminate unnecessary resources (such as operators or machinery) from a business environment by identifying a better process flow. This elimination of investment presents an additional method for generating a positive ROI from a simulation study. For example, assume that you are a purchasing manager who manages a team of purchasing agents (Figure 3-1). You are concerned that you have more agents than you need to achieve the objectives for your business unit. Rather than quickly reducing staff, you opt to simulate various strategies for changing the flow of purchasing paperwork through your team.

Your "as–is" purchasing configuration gets all orders placed on time, but your average staff utilization for all agents averages approximately 68%. Assuming the work day is typically 8 hours long, your staff averages 2½ hours of idle time! By using simulation, you are able to experiment with various alternatives for consolidating your purchasing processes so that they can be performed by fewer people. After reviewing the simulation model, you determine that an investment to train two members of your purchasing team to perform multiple activities allows you to continue to get all of your work done, decrease your average idle time from 32% to 8%, and eliminate two staff positions (Figure 3-2). At an annual cost of $50,000 per position, you immediately achieve a $100,000 savings.

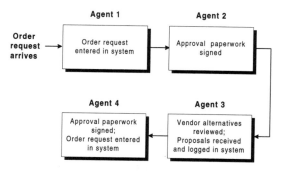

Figure 3-2 *Flow Diagram of "To-Be" Purchasing Configuration*

We have looked at three examples of quantifying simulation results in terms of savings on resource expenditures. The first example involved moving to a new system where we purchased the "right" amount of equipment rather than too much; the second example involved increasing our capacity commitment to generate savings in terms of our overall system performance; and the third example involved decreasing our resources (in this case, staff) by improving our business application's process flow. In all three examples, we were able to save money in the area of resource capacity and, consequently, improve our system's productivity.

▲ Resource Planning for New Facilities

Before we move on, let us take a closer look at the resource-planning application. Admittedly, in many situations, you will not be able to state objectively the savings you were able to recognize with simulation—and yet the use of the technology was critical in determining your recommendation. This often occurs when you are using simulation technology to size the resource capacity of a new facility that you are creating from scratch. In this application, the simulation model becomes a vehicle for exploring an entirely new layout configuration, process–flow strategy, and resource–sizing plan. And while the power that simulation delivers here is potentially significant, it is impossible to quantify, since you have no way of comparing the system strategy that the model helps you select against the one you would have selected without simulation.

Theoretically, you could conduct an additional nondynamic study to size the new plant configuration so that you would have a benchmark to compare against. Or, you might try to identify a similar business experience that was a total failure to compare against. But chances are, you will not have the time or desire to engage in such efforts simply to state the savings you have generated.

The question to ask yourself is, "What is it worth to identify the best solution to my problem the first time?" Not only are you identifying an optimal resource investment for your business, but you are also avoiding the trial–and–error method of system design that often occurs in the real world. Soon after you build a new facility or implement a new administrative process, you often identify significant problems that compromise your ability to meet your business objectives. For example, when introducing new products for manufacturing, many companies develop hardware prototypes and allow for lot sizes of one. They incur the unnecessary expense of making a single product and gain no appreciation for the way the manufacturing system will perform when forced to make products en masse. When the actual facility goes online for the initial time (without a simulation analysis), companies often experience dramatic problems in the form of late orders, excess inventory, and dissatisfied customers. All of this could have been avoided by simply creating a simulation model *before* system implementation.

In other situations, you can derive substantial value by selecting an appropriate balance of capacity with system performance. You may not have made up your mind to invest in additional resources to manage your business but you still want to explore the tradeoffs between investment and performance. Each scenario that you try in your model may present a unique ROI outcome. Eventually, you need to make a call on how much you are willing to spend to achieve your goals for your business.

▲ Inventory Management

Planning for resource investment or resource change is one method for evaluating the value of simulation. A second convenient method is to focus on savings that you may recognize by reducing the costs associated with managing inventory.

When running your business, you utilize resources to convert inputs to outputs for your customers. Your challenge is to place valuable resources in your system in such a way that they can perform their various functions (e.g., manufacture a product, speak to a customer, move materials, etc.) in a timely fashion. You need your entire operation to work in harmony so that you minimize circumstances where your inputs are not making quick progress on their way to becoming outputs. These delays are known as *bottlenecks*.

Bottlenecks exist in the form of customers waiting on hold to be serviced by customer-service agents. Bottlenecks exist as raw material or work in process (WIP) waiting on a shop floor to be manufactured by a machine. Bottlenecks exist in a variety of other forms such as cars in traffic and baggage waiting on a landing strip. Bottlenecks can kill a system's performance. Fortunately, most business managers are aware of this. Eli Goldratt's book *The Goal* (1984) helped awaken mainstream business professionals to the concept of bottleneck management. Goldratt's "Theory of Constraints" argues that, as a savvy business manager, you should solve problems within your facility by first eliminating, or at least pacifying, the most costly bottleneck before moving on to other system problems. With simulation technology, you can understand the impact of any proposed change on the bottleneck. As Goldratt suggests, you often "shift" the bottleneck from one location to the next, making your project a process of bottleneck chasing and extinguishing. Ultimately, you are diminishing your overall carrying cost.

A key issue in effectively managing your business is to realize that bottlenecks are expensive. The effective use of simulation can help you eliminate or reduce bottlenecks, thus saving you money.

To demonstrate the value of simulation in bottleneck analysis, I will expand on the simple manufacturing example presented earlier in this chapter. Simulation technology was used successfully to determine the right number of machines to purchase when we upgraded our system. Upon implementation, our 10 machines did an outstanding job of making our products efficiently. However, we are working for a dynamic, growing business, and a recent increase in orders has led to demands on our system that our current configuration cannot handle.

We have found that large amounts of WIP are accumulating in front of four of our most active machines. Not only are we losing our ability to make products in a timely and effective manner, we are also dramatically increasing our carrying cost of work-in-process inventory. This carrying cost is the money that is tied up in the inventory. Inventory that lies on our shop floor adds no value to our business. We need to convert raw materials into money-making product sales as quickly as possible.

Rather than immediately investing in additional equipment to solve our problem, we decide to explore a change in the process flow of our manufacturing system. We also start to use one of our machines to perform two different functions rather than only one. By using simulation, we are able to try out varying process-routing scenarios, and we identify a better way of managing our existing resources that lets us decrease our WIP carrying cost by 20% over a one-year period. Since our inventory is expensive, we are able to document a savings of $80,000. Suppose that our simulation effort only cost us $10,000—primarily in engineering time, since we already own the simulation software and have been trained in its use. In this example, we are able to document an ROI of 400%, expressed as the savings divided by our investment in analysis time.

In manufacturing examples, bottlenecks can be valued in terms of a carrying cost of work-in-process inventory. In many other application examples, bottlenecks are equally troublesome but are more difficult to quantify. In our market example, our objective was to eliminate bottlenecks that formed at our service counters. In the fast-food restaurant industry, bottlenecks again take the form of customers waiting to make a purchase. In the overnight-package-delivery business, a bottleneck could be the difference between shipping a package on time or not.

Quantifying the cost of bottlenecks in a customer-service application may be a bit more challenging than in manufacturing, but it can—and should—be done. For example, the cost of having people wait on hold to be serviced by a support professional is related to customers' tolerances for dealing with service delays. When customers decide that your company's service is unacceptable, they may switch to your competitor, and your cost becomes expressed in terms of lost business. Many companies place specific cost metrics on customer-service operations and consequently can quantify the results from a simulation study when the project leads to improvements in servicing customers.

▲ Speed-to-Market

In my experience in the simulation industry, I have observed many successful simulation projects. Most often the individuals involved have cited their successes on the basis of resource and/or inventory-related improvements. One friend—a simulation consultant—

operates according to the following motto: "If you have resource problems or bottlenecks, we have a solution for you." Typically, my friend uses simulation to address projects that align with his motto.

An often-overlooked benefit that simulation delivers is the facilitation of schedule reductions in the design, building, and start up of new business systems. The opportunity for companies to expedite their speed-to-market when launching new products can lead to a dramatic competitive advantage. Early markets command premium prices, such that a one-month schedule reduction can mean tens of millions of dollars in additional revenues in such industries as telecommunications, automotive, and semiconductor. Also, early manufacturing capacity often means new market share, which results in increased annual contributions to a corporation's overall profitability.

A simulation model of a new facility can become the very "backbone" of the entire start up phase. It becomes a test bed for evaluation of all proposed design and operating-philosophy changes. Early in the effort, simulation focuses the design team, thus eliminating wasted engineering design time. Throughout the effort, simulation keeps the team within the envelope of feasibility by quickly and consistently evaluating all proposed design alternatives. The objective here is expediency, flexibility, and communication throughout the project team.

In parallel to the design effort, the simulation model is used to determine all operational requirements for the new system, such as operator scheduling and preventive maintenance. All of this occurs before start up, maximizing the firm's opportunity for quick, effective, and profitable performance.

I am familiar with one firm that achieved as much as a 90% elimination in the overall start up time for a new facility by using simulation. The returns were in the many millions of dollars. Whether or not you achieve quite this level, simulation clearly provides the opportunity to generate quantifiable success when used to improve your company's speed-to-market.

▪ "Softer" Benefits of Simulation

It is always important to quantify the results of any business action you take. After all, every company needs to demonstrate an effective return on equity in order to remain in business. The use of simulation offers many benefits, however, that are challenging to express as a quantified ROI. These benefits are very compelling and do affect productivity and profits but in a more general way. We will now explore several of these "softer" benefits of using simulation.

▲ Getting to Know Your Business

During my career in the simulation industry, I have so often heard testimonials from simulation analysts that sound something like the following: "We purchased simulation technology to study a significant change that we planned to implement in our organization. The process of managing the simulation project forced us to gain a much deeper understanding of all the issues involved in making our final design decision. We derived value that far exceeded our investment in simulation technology by gaining this insight."

Simply put, the use of simulation forces you to get to know your business better than you ever did before. In order to create a model of a business application, you must first create a fundamental flow diagram of how decisions are made, how long it takes for processes to occur, how reliable your resources are, how often materials or phone calls come into your system, and on and on. The simulation project and simulation model bring to a focus all of your system behavior. As you conduct the project, you will need to interview various members of your staff in order to collect the information you need to complete a model. If you are modeling an "as-is" system, you will need to get out in the facility and gather information from your actual operation. If you are modeling a new site or new business configuration, you will need to work with individuals in your enterprise (or with your suppliers) to get the best information that your experience can generate.

With your entire organization or department working toward a common goal (i.e., to complete a successful simulation analysis), chances are good that you will identify areas for improvement within your business well before you have completed your simulation study. Working together as a project team, you communicate with each other more effectively and learn more about your entire business operation. I often hear of "on-the-fly" problem solving that takes place as simulation-project participants get to know what is going on in their business environments.

▲ Minimizing Risk

When you buy a house or expensive jewelry, it is common practice to purchase an insurance policy to protect your investment. The price you pay is low considering the stress you would otherwise experience, knowing how much a fire, theft, or accident could cost you.

The use of simulation technology also serves as an insurance policy—in this case, against potentially costly implementation errors. These errors may take the form of insufficient staffing, a flawed maintenance strategy, or an inventory policy that cripples your ability to respond to customer orders quickly and efficiently. These system flaws may cost you valuable business, market share, and morale in your facilities. When it is used properly, simulation technology delivers a highly accurate prediction of how your system will perform, once it goes online. The confidence you gain from running a computerized model of your system prior to implementation may in itself be worth your entire investment in the technology—especially if the change you are facilitating with simulation is strategic and/or high investment in nature.

Simulation models allow you to create imaginary worlds so that you can test things that you would never try in real life. You can try implementation scenarios that you may consider to be higher risk (since they differ greatly from traditional practice). You may find yourself stumbling upon a "to-be" scenario that clearly outperforms all others. Without a simulation model, you would never have arrived at such an effective implementation option. In this context, simulation unleashes the opportunity for you to get creative in your "what-if" analysis while delivering an invaluable insurance policy against business scenarios that could lead you to a damaging, costly disappointment.

▲ The Role of Animation

Another compelling capability that is exploited in most commercial simulation products on the market today is animation. Many of the leading simulation vendors provide a fairly easy way for simulation analysts to create high-quality graphical representations of their models. "Cartoons" of factories, airports, and warehouse environments make it very easy to present project ideas to a broad audience of individuals whose input is significant to the project, without requiring them to become skilled in the simulation tool or to understand detailed simulation results (Figure 3-3).

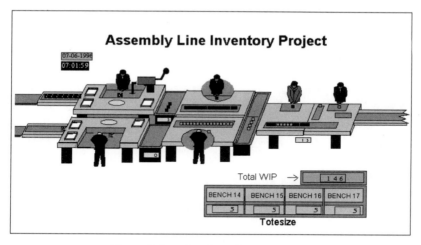

Figure 3-3 *Animation of Assembly Line*

The opportunity to use animation as part of a simulation study adds tremendous value to the technology and its application. Suddenly, a simulation–project manager can engage many levels of management, facility-level employees (on the shop floor or within the administrative world), and his co-analysts in the project. Since any project of strategic significance to an organization requires appropriate "buy-in" from all key personnel, animation is critical as a vehicle to facilitate this process as well as total project communication.

When it comes time for the simulation-project manager to make a strong recommendation based on the findings of his simulation analysis, he can leverage the animation to gain instant credibility for his project and his project proposal. He can allow his management team to watch as the proposed "to-be" system executes before their eyes. He will also be able to use the animation in order to educate employees at a facility level on the benefits of making a system change. In this case, the animation may become a vehicle for training facility-level employees in the effective management of new business processes.

The use of animation as a presentation tool works well on the back end of a project—to make a compelling recommendation—but it also can be used to sell the concept of evaluating a problem in the first place. Often, organizations are reluctant to change a business initiative that has been relatively successful. Their operation may be generating a profit, their customers may be satisfied, and all appears to be well. However, a very significant opportunity to upgrade their operation and increase profits may be hiding in the form of a few key changes. In this case, simulation—in conjunction with an impressive animation—can be used to illustrate the potential effect of a system change on a company's bottom line.

▲ Avoiding Physical Experiments

Frequently, the value of simulation is expressed by identifying the headaches that it can help you to avoid. One such headache, for example, arises in exploring various business scenarios by conducting physical experiments within your actual facility. You move resources around in your business and vary other conditions, such as order size and the sequence of your process flow, to understand what actually occurs under varying circumstances.

I have heard stories about how the airline industry used to hire college students to walk through their ticket counters during the middle of the night in order to understand the effect of various ticket-agent staffing policies on customer service. In other cases, companies have built tabletop material handling systems that are miniature versions of the actual facility, and fast-food restaurants often operate full-scale restaurants for experimentation with new products and services.

Whether you are conducting physical simulations as a strategy or you are making mistakes in your business by implementing configurations and process flows that are not effective, you are investing time and money in activities that could have been simulated within an imaginary system living inside your personal computer.

▲ A "Differentiator" for Professional-Services Firms

Professional-services firms can leverage simulation technology as a way to differentiate their service offerings from their competitors. For example, in the architectural engineering business, the difference between Firm A's proposal and Firm B's may be that Firm A offers to deliver a dynamic simulation model of the recommended facility layout. This suggests that Firm A attempts to optimize the performance of the process and builds a perfectly matched facility. The simulation model can have continuing value to the customer as changes are periodically considered for improving the operation. For example, after landing the job, Firm A may test out various business scenarios within the simulation model, so that their client can participate in making a decision on the amount of excess capacity that is required to facilitate expansion.

The use of simulation as a front-to-back selling, engineering analysis, and delivery methodology clearly represents a way for professional-services firms to gain a strategic advantage. The use of simulation in consulting engagements also becomes an enabling technology allowing firms to express a "value proposition" or to participate in "risk sharing." Many of the world's leading management consulting firms offer to charge clients for a percentage of the savings they are able to generate rather than for the time and travel of their consultants. By effectively utilizing simulation, services organizations can work closely with their clients to find the best implementation scenario while quantifying specific savings derived from change-management projects.

▲ Operational Decision Support

When you implement simulation as a fundamental methodology for managing your business applications, you will begin to derive additional value from the technology over time.

Chances are, initially you will use the technology as a vehicle for facilitating a strategic decision. Simulation is typically introduced to a firm when a major change is forthcoming. This might involve the construction of a new facility or design of a new customer-service center. The output from your simulation model may support a multimillion-dollar investment in facilities, equipment, and staff. Once you have implemented the simulation-enabled business configuration, however, you should make certain that you do not relegate your model to the shelf. Unfortunately, this often occurs today—even in companies that are recognizing a very positive ROI from their simulation-project work. Your best investment is to "keep the model alive" by periodically upgrading it to match the current status of your business. In this way, you can explore hypothetical changes to your business on an ongoing basis.

Suppose that you could understand the effects of changes in your customers' order requirements—what would be the value to your enterprise? What if you could look continually into the future to understand where your business will be in one week, one month, or one year? The use of simulation as an operational decision support tool will allow your business to manage itself on an ongoing basis, giving full attention to the dynamics inside everyday operations.

Simulation can influence how orders are placed, scheduled, and controlled. You can take today's orders and system status and quickly fast-forward in time to understand how your business will operate relative to your objectives. By making appropriate on-the-fly decisions, you can effectively reduce operator and machine idle time. When you consider that operator idle time runs as high as 90% and machine idle time as high as 23% in some manufacturing applications, such a reduction can be truly dramatic.

As you begin using simulation as an institutionalized decision-support methodology, you enable yourself to answer the question "What if?" quickly and effectively. For example, if you are analyzing an entire supply chain, you need to understand immediately the impact that a missed delivery of raw materials to one of your manufacturing facilities will have on your ability to hit your customer-order due dates. Without a model that adequately captures system variability and decision logic, you cannot answer this question with a high enough degree of confidence. Simulation combines quick-response capability with the accuracy required to support significant decisions. The decisions that stem from your simulation analysis may involve additional capacity investment, shuffling of current priorities, or warning your customer of a potential problem in sufficient time to take appropriate action.

In business today, we need to invest in tools and technologies that allow us to state the benefits of change concisely. The potential that simulation offers for you to demonstrate a very positive ROI in your business applications is significant. This chapter has focused on why you should use simulation in terms of the specific value that it adds to your business. Chapter 4 will help you identify the applications and markets within which simulation has been widely accepted and applied. You will learn about how some of the world's leading companies are successfully deploying this exciting technology and will add to your understanding of when and where it makes sense to apply simulation.

Simulation: A Technology for the Mainstream

Great innovations should not be forced on slender majorities.

THOMAS JEFFERSON

Simply put, simulation is emerging as a mainstream problem-solving technology. It is evolving from specialized use only by individuals who are highly focused and highly skilled into widespread use by business analysts and engineers, who include it in their everyday problem-solving toolbox.

This chapter profiles the growth in acceptance of simulation by various industries over the past three decades leading up to today. In reading this development, you will also gain insight into the specific applications for which simulation is being used. Many of today's leading companies have commented on both the level of enthusiasm they have generated within their firms and the specific types of business problems they are addressing with simulation.

Organizations today are making enterprise-level commitments to simulation technology at an accelerating pace. According to a late 1996 study by *Manufacturing Systems* magazine, discrete manufacturers would spend $336 million on simulation software in 1997, a 106% increase over the $166 million they spent in 1995. A separate informal study conducted by Gartner Group (Stamford, Conn.) in 1995, focused on business process reengineering tools, stated that "most BPR efforts and process improvement initiatives can benefit from at least basic simulation technology, and it should be used by all organizational types." The study cited that only "1 in 10" of those involved with BPR efforts were using simulation. Ken Kleinberg, research director of Gartner Group, stated possible reasons for such low adoption as a general lack of familiarity with the technique on the part of most business analysts and the fact that it required a proactive step. However, the potential for payback is significant. Gartner believes that the simulation/animation market will continue to grow and that by 1998 the use of the technology on BPR projects will probably have doubled to 20%. And while the total market size for simulation is hard to nail down, what is clear is that both the market size and the number of successful applications of this technology are growing strongly.

◼ The Making of a Mainstream Technology

In the information-technology business, many tools and technologies that are valuable to some practitioners have been ignored by many others. Neural networking and artificial intelligence are prime examples. Each generated a tremendous amount of enthusiasm when first released, and each attracted a large following of technologists who committed themselves to spreading usage and application on a large scale.

Neural networking, which was first released in the 1980s, involves using computer-based technology that can train itself based on feedback it receives. Artificial intelligence, a similarly smart information technology, provides automated decision-making potential. Both still exist but are clearly outside the mainstream.

In *Crossing the Chasm* (1991), Geoffrey Moore presents a "Technology Adoption Life Cycle" which characterizes the growth of information technology markets. According to Moore, a technology reaches the mainstream market when it successfully jumps across the "chasm" between the early adopters (the technologists) and the early majority (the pragmatists). The early majority—which makes up approximately one-third of the total market for any information technology according to Moore—represents the beginning of the mainstream. The mainstream market is generally dramatically larger (often several orders of magnitude) than the early adopting market.

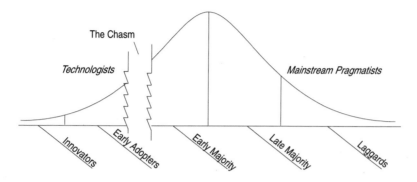

Figure 4-1 *Technology Adoption Life Cycle*

Most new information technologies never make it across Moore's chasm. In spite of large investments by organizations and the early adopter community, the tools never gain quite enough acceptance to become mainstream. Getting across the chasm is challenging for various reasons:

▼ Pragmatists are not willing to invest greatly in high-risk technologies.

▼ Pragmatists do not consider technologists to be credible.

▼ Pragmatists are very price sensitive.

▼ Pragmatists want to buy "standardized" technologies.

Neural networking and artificial intelligence failed to cross the chasm because they could not be marketed effectively to the pragmatists. The technologists' excitement about the tools was not enough to push them over the chasm and into the mainstream.

On the other hand, many information technologies have successfully landed in the lucrative mainstream market. Examples are the spreadsheet, presentation tools such as Microsoft® PowerPoint®

and Lotus® Freelance, various internet technologies such as the browser, and business-diagramming software. Each tool first captured the technologists as customers before capturing millions of pragmatic users who accepted it as a standardized way of doing business.

Simulation is now emerging out of the chasm and into the mainstream. It had been caught in the chasm for roughly three decades for various reasons, such as:

▼ It was very difficult for everyday practitioners to use.

▼ It was very expensive (price of software, time required to use).

▼ Organizations were not aware of its value.

▼ The vendors supplying simulation technology were small and at times unstable (increasing the risk of investment).

Today, times have changed. Recent developments in simulation-software technology have made the tools much easier to use. This ease of use has been complemented by advanced operating systems, such as Microsoft® Windows 95® and Windows NT®, which make simulation analysts more productive. Also increasing productivity is the fact that simulation users can now integrate their modeling applications with other standard desktop technologies, such as spreadsheets. And, the price of acquiring simulation software and related hardware has decreased substantially, making it easier for organizations to justify their initial investment.

☑ Lower price (of software and hardware)
☑ Ease of use
☑ Improved operating systems (e.g., Microsoft® Windows 95®, Windows NT®)
☑ Faster PC's
☑ Integration with desktop tools (e.g., spreadsheets, business diagramming)
☑ Management-level acceptance and enthusiasm

Figure 4-2 *Factors Contributing to Simulation's Widespread Growth*

Perhaps the most significant change in the simulation market over the past few years has been the rapid acceptance of the technology by organizations throughout the world. Companies that previously did not use it to facilitate decision making are doing so today in great numbers. Managers are advocating its use across the entire enterprise— for manufacturing, distribution, warehousing, office applications, and supply-chain management. As more and more organizations recognize its potential for saving money and increasing productivity, simulation technology is spreading throughout the business community at a rapid pace.

Let us now examine how some of the world's largest governments, industries, premiere organizations, and universities are applying simulation technology to manage change.

▄ A Raving Fan of Simulation Technology—The ▲ United States Government

An early adopter of simulation technology and a very solid advocate of the market has been the United States government. The technology was first embraced by the government for conducting military strategic planning back in the early 1960s. More recently, the level of support for simulation by the U.S. government has grown substantially. In 1991, the United States Department of Defense identified simulation as one of the "Critical Technologies for the 21st Century." The report, filed by the National Critical Technologies Panel, describes 22 technologies considered "essential for the United States to develop in the interests of the nation's long-term security and economic prosperity." This report was followed up by a similar one in 1996, again citing simulation as essential.

A project entitled "Next-Generation Manufacturing" (NGM) funded by the U.S. Department of Energy, Department of Defense, National Institute of Standards and Technology, and the National Science Foundation—with participants from more than 50 leading

U.S. companies and universities—conducted research over 15 months (in 1996 and 1997) to develop specific recommendations for future manufacturing enterprises. NGM's executive report calls for "pervasive modeling and simulation" for all organizations.

According to the program directive, "Modeling and simulation will reflect a new way of doing business rather than a supporting technology. All production decisions will be made on the basis of modeling and simulation methods, rather than on build and test methods. Modeling and simulation tools will move from being in the domain of the technologist to being a tool for all involved in the product realization, production, and business process."

Simulation has been widely deployed by the U.S. Department of Defense (DoD) for modeling battlefield logistics and medical field support. Defense contractors, such as Boeing, Lockheed Martin, and Rockwell, routinely use simulation to analyze the manufacturing of defense weapons and related supplies. According to a recent strategic planning study undertaken by the DoD, "A $20 million investment in enhancing its current simulation capabilities can, with full implementation, reduce total DoD and private industry manufacturing costs by as much as $1.3 billion a year." Today, manufacturing companies are using the technology on a widespread basis. Organizations across the entire sector rely upon simulation for managing change as part of their standard business methodology.

Enthusiastic government support for simulation technology does not end in the United States. The governments of many other countries are investing in simulation technology as a way of making government agencies and business more competitive. A highly visible multinational example is a research initiative called Intelligent Manufacturing Systems (IMS). The IMS program, first proposed by Japan in 1989, today has six participating regions—Japan, Australia, Canada, the European community, five European Free Trade Association countries, and the United States. Its objective is "to develop and integrate the best ideas on advanced manufacturing systems into the next generation of manufacturing systems." The program is attempting to "provide a vision and structure for worldwide sharing of manufacturing technology development, including costs, risks, and benefits, in a balanced and equitable manner."

The IMS program has identified simulation as a core technology upon which manufacturing enterprises must be created and managed. It is one of the program's seven primary areas of focus (technical task areas). IMS calls for "an integratable set of simulation models merging a bottom-up view of the factory floor with a top-down view of the globally distributed virtual enterprise." A key issue is the agility of manufacturing firms or their ability to thrive in the face of unpredicted change.

Many of the government-led initiatives to increase investment in simulation technology have occurred in concert with the world's leading commercial organizations in the manufacturing and services sectors. As a means for examining the many different industries that have embraced simulation technology, I will begin with those who adopted the tool early and will move through other examples of industries that are only starting to realize the value of simulation technology.

▲ Where Simulation Was Born—The Manufacturing Sector

When I began my career in the simulation industry in 1987, nearly all of the organizations using the technology were in the manufacturing sector. Although a few users would appear in such services industries as health care and logistics, most companies that had accepted the technology with any level of enthusiasm were evaluating manufacturing systems.

The early acceptance of simulation in manufacturing occurred for a number of reasons. One reason had to do with the frequency of change in products and processes within manufacturing and the continual need to redesign facility layouts. Another reason was that manufacturing systems in the 1960s and 1970s were better suited for simulation technology than service industries because they were more clearly defined and formalized in terms of their procedures. Today, however, the service industries have invested such a tremendous amount in formalizing and systematizing all business processes, such as customer support, purchasing procedures, and order processing, that this disparity no longer exists. According to J. H. Harrington (*Business Process Improvement*), "It has been observed that 80% of all business processes are repetitive processes that can benefit from the same analysis techniques used to improve manufacturing systems."

Still another reason that simulation was widely used in manufacturing was that nearly all of the early success stories came out of manufacturing. Manufacturing professionals gave all of the technical papers at trade shows. Simulation vendors focused their energies on manufacturing companies by developing software features that were aimed at manufacturing applications. All of this focused activity going on inside the manufacturing sector gave the technology some level of momentum and allowed it to establish itself as an exciting niche market.

Many of the early adopters of simulation technology back in the 1960s and early 1970s were from the metals and aerospace industries. These industries commonly hired highly skilled research professionals to develop mainframe-based simulation models. Programming languages such as FORTRAN were often used to model manufacturing processes. One steel firm back in the early 1970s maintained a staff of nine Ph.D. research professionals to simulate their slab and caster applications. Not only were the costs incurred to employ such talent high, but the cost to run the simulation models on large mainframes ranged from $600 to $1,000 per hour. In spite of what may seem like exorbitant expenses, organizations were, in many cases, recognizing a very positive ROI, as they were commonly facilitating multimillion-dollar investment decisions.

Simulation technology continued to gain momentum in the 1970s and early 1980s in the manufacturing sector. Computers were becoming faster and less expensive, and the value of simulation was recognized by other industries such as automotive, electronics, and consumer appliances. In spite of an increased level of awareness, simulation was not viewed as a core part of most organizations' business methodology. Often, it was used only to rescue a very problematic situation rather than to design a new system or plan a facility upgrade.

In the 1990s, simulation technology is becoming commonplace throughout the manufacturing sector. In most leading firms, it is no longer an optional technology. Many organizations have made it a standardized methodology for managing change and for running their business. Manufacturing firms use simulation in order to save money, make informed decisions, and remain competitive. Many manufacturers now require their suppliers to utilize the technology in order to ensure that they are buying products that have been produced in a cost-effective manner. Let us now explore how some of the world's leading manufacturing industries and organizations are leveraging simulation technology to manage change.

◼ Simulation in the Aerospace Industry

With the high degree of support for simulation technology demonstrated by the U.S. government, it stands to reason that U.S. defense contractors would follow suit by using the technology to improve systems they were managing for their government customers. The aerospace industry was the first commercial community to embrace the technology industrywide back in the 1960s and early 1970s. Simulation models of assembly, repair, and maintenance processes for the manufacture of fighter planes, missiles, helicopters, and space-launch vehicles were under development several decades ago and continue to prevail throughout the industry. The technology has become a vehicle for cost savings in manufacturing, and it has proven to be an outstanding communication tool for project management and for coordination with various government agencies.

McDonnell Douglas Corporation

At revenues of $13.8 billion, McDonnell Douglas Corporation[1] (MDC) is one of the world's leading aerospace and defense companies. MDC designs, develops, manufactures, integrates, and supports military and commercial aircraft, helicopters, missiles, space-launch vehicles, and other space systems. Simulation activity at MDC dates back to the 1970s; however, the tool gained true momentum as a strategic technology in the mid-1980s.

Initial projects at MDC were focused on throughput analysis for assembly, maintenance, and repair of its products. Industrial engineers conducted most of the initial simulation–project activity, often facilitating high-impact decisions regarding facility-layout changes to improve manufacturing productivity and performance.

Within the last five years, a new environment has emerged within the aerospace industry, driven largely by the Air Force Virtual Manufacturing initiative. The emphasis of projects at MDC has subsequently grown to include two distinct groups: one that continues to use simulation for traditional production improvement and layout projects, and a second that applies the technology extensively during the proposal and preproduction phase of new contracts.

One project was conducted on the manufacture of the C-17 Globemaster III, an airlift that allows the U.S. Air Force to carry large combat equipment and troops or humanitarian aid across international distances. The model—which focused on evaluating the cost impact of various delivery scenarios—was used by the Air Force in an effort to gain Congressional approval for the seven-year $14.2 billion contract with MDC.

---

[1] Boeing's acquisition of McDonnell Douglas was finalized during production of this book.

The simulation effort provided a valuable methodology for demonstrating the cost and benefits of the delivery schedule that was accepted.

An additional successful application of simulation for addressing the preproduction phase occurred when MDC analysts simulated the Joint Direct Attack Munition (JDAM). The JDAM project is aimed at converting existing free-fall bombs to become "smart" munitions. A model—which captured several tiers of the project supply chain—was accepted by the Air Force in lieu of a traditional manufacturing plan. When MDC was debriefed on why they were selected for the JDAM program, they were informed that the simulation results gave the Air Force confidence that the MDC-proposed price was realistic. MDC was consequently awarded a $70 million pilot project that could result in upward of $2 billion in orders since the U.S. Department of Defense intends to purchase 87,496 JDAM's by the early years of the 21st century.

According to James Rossie, team leader of MDC's Virtual Manufacturing initiative, "Simulation has now been institutionalized across the organization as a standard way of doing business." Jim cites that MDC "has recognized dramatic benefits from using the technology" and that "some of the firm's prototype models have resulted in a 90% reduction in engineering changes."

A key area for future simulation growth within the industry is the problem that faces the aerospace industry in the area of product pricing. "Simulation is the most viable tool that will eventually take us to a cost estimate that can be verified and validated and be responsive to continuing changes in product and rate. Historically, the industry has created cost estimates for multibillion-dollar contracts on the basis of dollars per pound." According to James, "There is a significant paradigm shift that has occurred in terms of how many people it takes to design a new product. Simulation technology will allow us to model the entire process to derive an accurate cost estimate."

▲ Simulation in the Automotive Industry

No industry has embraced simulation technology as aggressively as the automotive industry. Every major player in the automotive market has made simulation a key methodology for managing its business. In addition to embracing the technology, the auto industry, in some cases, has mandated that simulation be used by the supplier community. Simulation applications within the automotive industry include various assembly, welding, and painting operations. Non-manufacturing applications such as parts distribution and product-development processes are also simulated. Most automotive firms also use simulation widely to design and modify new systems.

Simulation in Action

Ford Motor Company

An early adopter of simulation technology in the automotive industry was Ford Motor Company. When simulation was first introduced at Ford, it was used only by "experts." As a result, its potential reach throughout the organization was limited by the availability of expert users. Often it was used only as a last resort and received minimal senior-management approval.

Today, simulation receives significant support from Ford's division general managers and sector vice presidents, who understand its value and promote its use. The company has developed its own internal simulation methodology on how to conduct successful simulation projects. Monthly simulation training courses are offered at the Ford Motor Company Training and Development Center for all interested employees, and all managers who move through Ford's internal management training programs are exposed to and trained in the use of simulation technology.

Among various manufacturing applications, Ford uses simulation as a "prototype" tool for production systems in order to understand the interactions among various system components and to determine adequate system requirements. Simulation helps to improve investment efficiency, reduce operating cost, and reduce lead time. The savings in 116 recently monitored cases are rather substantial—ranging from 5% to 22% of the total manufacturing investment for a facility or project. This does not include the frequent lead-time reductions (of up to two months per project).

Dr. Hwa-Sung Na is a technical specialist in Ford's Advanced Manufacturing Technology Department. She has been coordinating much of Ford's simulation effort for the past 10 years, and her knowledge of Ford's simulation effort goes back to the 1960s. According to Dr. Na, "Due to the many improvements that have occurred in both hardware and software platforms, we can now provide this technology to any analyst who has an interest. Thus, we see much wider usage of simulation at an earlier state of development, and we routinely reap much more substantial benefits."

Simulation technology has spread throughout virtually every manufacturing sector at Ford. And there is no indication that the momentum will slow any time soon. Dr. Na believes that in the future, "Simulation will most likely become as common as Microsoft® Excel, installed as a standard tool on every PC. People will feel far more comfortable in discussing the statistical aspects of the analysis, and simulation will become an everyday decision-support tool for all levels of workers."

▲ Simulation in the Electronics Industry

Also an early adopter of simulation, the electronics industry probably is the second most engaged community of simulation practitioners. Electronics firms incur frequent modification to manufacturing environments due to extremely short product life cycles and rapid industry change. Prices in the industry decline quickly, forcing continuous improvement and increased productivity. For example, the personal-computer market has averaged a 10% price drop per month in recent years. In the pager business, prices have dropped approximately 15% per year. Manufacturing firms producing semiconductors, computers, printed circuit boards, communication systems, and various other types of electronics products are widely deploying simulation technology to manage the rapid change that is taking place in their business environments.

Simulation in Action

Motorola

In spite of failed ad hoc efforts to introduce simulation at Motorola back in the 1970s, the technology gained the acceptance and enthusiasm of senior management in 1987. The event that led to this management support was a very large semiconductor facility that did not work well. Simulation technology came to the rescue.

Following the high-visibility semiconductor project, simulation emerged on the scene in the late 1980s as a standard way of solving business problems. In 1988 and 1989 at Motorola University in Schaumburg, Ill., approximately 30 managers were trained per month on the concept and value of simulation technology. The 500 managers who received simulation training as part of a two-week information-technology exercise helped the organization build a strong foundation of believers in simulation.

Today, more than 1,000 employees at Motorola have successfully completed some level of simulation training. Simulation technology is very visible with CEO Christopher Galvin on board as a vocal supporter. Hundreds of simulation projects are performed each year ranging from two-day studies to much larger-scale multiple-month initiatives. Only a few individuals at Motorola are full-time simulation analysts—most of the users of the technology utilize simulation on a part-time basis alongside various other decision-enabling tools.

Motorola's enthusiasm level for the technology became so high at one point that the company created its own simulator called MASCOT (Motorola Artificial Simulation Companion Organizer and Teacher). The tool received most of its use at Motorola University as a training tool, where it helped the instructors simplify the key concepts of simulation for managers.

According to John Liang, a senior manager who oversees Motorola's Enterprise Modeling and Analysis team, "Senior management has been very excited by the results of simulation since we have been able to demonstrate dramatic return on our investment in the areas of throughput improvement, cycle-time reduction, and general cost avoidance." John's group has the responsibility of assisting with new projects and transferring the technology to field operations where simulation is practiced.

John cites one example project where Motorola conducted a simulation study of a low-orbit-satellite-making supply-chain operation known as IRIDIUM. In this project—where Motorola teamed with defense contractors Lockheed Martin and Raytheon—a $1.5 million savings in inventory reduction was achieved because of the simulation study. An additional $500,000 was saved when the model identified an implementation scenario that would help avoid the acquisition of expensive satellite transportation equipment. Motorola experienced various other benefits from the study in the areas of negotiating contracts with suppliers and communicating ideas to all parties involved in the project. "We will continue to invest heavily in simulation technology as an enterprise since its usage directly improves our bottom line," says John.

Manufacturing or Service?... The Answer Is— Both

While the large majority of the early applications for simulation occurred in the manufacturing sector, the growth in technology acceptance within the services sector actually began in the manufacturing sector itself. Many of the early adopters of simulation began to apply the technologies for such projects as reengineering purchasing systems, designing warehousing and distribution strategies, and various other nonmanufacturing applications. Ambitious engineers who were already saving their companies money on manufacturing projects stimulated the use of simulation outside of the traditional environment.

Simulation in Action

Nike, Inc.

Nike, Inc., is the world's leading designer and marketer of athletic footwear, apparel, and accessories with $6 billion in sales. The popular company has made a significant commitment to simulation technology for managing changes to its warehousing and distribution centers. Having experienced dramatic growth over the last several years, Nike has undergone many expansions and new-facility construction in locations throughout the world. Simulation has been successfully applied to many projects in Beaverton, Ore. (Nike's headquarters); Memphis, Tenn.; and at sites in Belgium and Australia. New facilities in Japan and Korea will also be modeled.

Pat Busbee, a senior industrial engineer with Nike, first introduced simulation technology to the company in 1991 during a continuous-process improvement (CPI) initiative. The firm originally used flowcharts to communicate ideas under the CPI program. According to Pat, "Simulation helped bring the flowcharts to life. Plus, the dynamic animation proved to be much more effective in communicating ideas than static charts and graphs. Simulation was an immediate hit."

The first simulation application at Nike immediately saved the company $20,000 per year when two workcenters for labeling new cartons in a Memphis receiving dock were consolidated into one. The model not only helped identify a more efficient method for handling the labeling function, but it also proved to be an excellent vehicle for training and communicating with floor supervisors who manage the daily operation.

Since the introduction of simulation at Nike, the technology has become a standard fixture. Top-level management has enthusiastically embraced it. Pat claims that, "We are now doing simulation as an everyday practice. Several years ago this would not have been possible, but with the power of today's PC's and the advent of easy-to-use software, we can build models quickly and frequently."

One of the most successful projects at Nike occurred in 1995 in Belgium when a model helped save the company more than $500,000. The simulation effort helped Nike's analysts identify a theory of operation where a high-speed sorter was slowed and synchronized with a dynamic packing station so that the desired throughput could be achieved. The result allowed the company to forgo an unneeded investment in accumulation conveyor capacity.

Nike does not utilize centralized engineering departments. Rather, project teams form to analyze and remedy design and implementation problems. Each team generally encompasses various engineering and analysis disciplines. Simulation initially became part of a Memphis distribution project team and is now spreading more widely across the organization, so that its value can be leveraged for many additional projects.

▲ The Services Sector

Given that the services sector represents 80% of the world's combined Gross Domestic Product, it is important for any emerging technology to find a home within nonmanufacturing firms. Within the last five years, simulation has begun to gain wider acceptance in the services world, and there is tremendous upside potential for new applications in this sector.

Services industries vary in terms of their present-day acceptance of simulation technology for a variety of reasons. One reason is that many services organizations do not have the information-technology support structure that manufacturing companies do. Without it, the use of simulation technology was too challenging for them. Some early success stories in the services sector occurred when companies hired consultants to do simulation studies for them.

An additional factor was that nearly all of the simulation-software and consulting firms directed their attention toward the technologist community in manufacturing. Product features, educational materials, and trade shows primarily accommodated the needs of the manufacturers, leaving the services firms unawakened to the new technology.

Today, services firms are benefiting from easier-to-use simulation tools and management's awareness of the technology's value. Companies in the simulation-technology business are providing tools and services that specifically cater to their needs. Organizations in the logistics, health care, telecommunications, and financial industries are embracing the technology at an accelerating pace. While the services business may lack the large number of successful and committed practitioners that the manufacturing sector has created, there is no lack of opportunity for application and growth of simulation throughout the services world.

▲ Simulation in the Logistics Industry

Logistics describes a variety of different industries and application areas. Technically speaking, it is the process of strategically managing the movement and storage of materials, parts, and finished inventory from the supplier, through the firm, and on to customers. Organizations themselves may move the items, or they may hire outside parties to facilitate the movement.

Simulation is used broadly by organizations dealing with logistics problems for process improvement. Many leading firms that offer logistics services use the technology to improve their operations—beginning with the activities that occur at centralized "hub" sites where packages are sorted and routed to their appropriate destinations and moving up to the entire distribution system. The technology helps to identify appropriate resource configurations to sort and transport the goods most quickly from one location to the next. It also helps organizations zero in on specific costs associated with performing the logistics function.

Simulation in Action

United Parcel Service (UPS)

United Parcel Service (UPS) is the world's largest package distribution company, transporting more than 3.1 billion parcels and documents annually with sales greater than $22 billion. Mike Eskew, currently vice president of Engineering at UPS, introduced simulation to the company in 1987. At the time, Mike invested in the technology to analyze the unloading and loading of aircraft at the UPS hub in Louisville. The model allowed the company to understand various dependencies in the system and helped them immediately save $45,000 in avoiding an expensive retrofit. From that point, simulation emerged on the scene as a key technology for UPS.

As the Airline Group was achieving its initial success with simulation, an additional team at Roadnet Technologies, the Baltimore-based subsidiary of UPS, launched a simulation effort to place the technology in the hands of dispatch managers at the UPS hub sites throughout the United States. The application—known as "Shifter Sim"—allowed field managers to make changes in shift schedules to better utilize their employees and to avoid adding additional staff. More than 80 UPS hub sites soon began using simulation to understand the impact of varying staff schedules on the efficiencies of their operations.

Today, simulation has become a standard way of doing business at UPS. Senior-level management, such as Phil Hunter, vice president of United Parcel Service's Airline Industrial Engineering Group, are staunch advocates of the technology. According to Operations Research Manager Gregory Reinhardt, who oversees a staff of simulation analysts, "Our employees today are more familiar with simulation. Many of them learned how to use the technology in school, and the overall level of awareness of the technology's potential for savings is much greater." Greg claims that today's projects are more plentiful, larger in scale, and often more complex than the firm's early applications.

Greg notes that his simulation team's models have, on numerous occasions, saved upward of $200,000 per project. Savings have generally been realized in the form of avoided expenditures, although simulation has demonstrated value in a number of other ways. For example, when working with a conveyor supplier in Europe, UPS used a simulation model to negotiate the specifications of the conveyor design. The simulation gave the project manager confidence that the system would work, and it helped assure that the supplier's specifications were optimized to UPS's preference.

Simulation advocates at UPS have invested in educating other employees on the value of simulation. The technology receives significant publicity in the form of internal corporate communications on the company intranet and in the firm's biweekly newspaper. Moreover, the consistently successful projects and frequent internal one-on-one training have helped increase awareness throughout the firm.

When asked to point out the most significant benefit of using simulation, Greg talks about the insurance policy that the technology delivers to the firm's most senior executives. "When we are designing a new multimillion-dollar operation, simulation allows our executive steering committee to sign on the dotted line with a higher degree of confidence."

◼ Simulation in the Transportation Industry

Airlines, railroads, mass-transit systems, and other related businesses are using simulation technology to evaluate transportation systems effectively. From an application standpoint, the simulation models are very similar to logistics problems, the primary exception being that the transported items are people instead of goods. Simulation technology allows organizations in the transportation industry to understand the impact of changing schedules, the utilization of transportation vehicles, total transportation time, and travel cost. At times the technology is applied to study the behavior of an entire airport operation or railroad switching yard to evaluate competing configuration alternatives, and it is also being applied to other diverse problems such as staffing for reservations centers.

Simulation in Action

AMR Corporation

In the airline industry, AMR (the parent of American Airlines) has been an aggressive user of simulation technology since the early 1980s. First introduced as a technology for assessing a taxiway design at the San Juan International Airport, simulation technology has become a widely used tool for evaluating baggage-handling systems, determining ticket-agent staffing requirements, assessing airport passenger flow, and designing entirely new airport terminals.

Tom McArdle is vice president at SABRE Technology Solutions^{SM}, The SABRE Group's information technology (IT) division, a subsidiary of AMR. Tom first introduced simulation to SABRE and now oversees a team of more than 30 analysts who perform simulation and related projects. His group conducts approximately 10% of their projects for AMR and the other 90% for clients such as airport authorities (e.g., Dallas/ Ft. Worth International Airport, the British Airport Authority, and Airport de Paris) and civil and aviation authorities (e.g., Federal Aviation Administration). In addition to modeling airline and airport systems, The SABRE Group has also successfully applied simulation technology for customers in the railroad business such as the German Federal Railroad in Berlin, the proposed Texas High-Speed Rail System, and the Las Vegas People-Mover System.

According to Tom, "Simulation is nearly the only means to evaluate transportation systems because of the inherent complexities and high volume of passengers. All of the industry leaders in our business have come to the conclusion that simulation is the only way to make accurate predictions and to facilitate design decisions effectively." Customers of The SABRE Group, such as the many airport authorities, are beginning to mandate that simulation technology be applied to all new facility design projects. This has helped the modeling team at The SABRE Group to grow rapidly.

One of The SABRE Group's recent projects was to build a simulation model of London Heathrow's proposed fifth passenger terminal (T5). T5 is planned to be a state-of-the-art facility with integrated rail services, including the existing London Underground and the proposed mainline express service to the city. During the analysis, The SABRE Group used future flight schedules (which included aircraft with 600-plus seats) to estimate demand on T5's people-mover system and baggage-handling system. The British Airport Authority (BAA) suggested several proposed designs for the systems within T5. Based on the results generated from the simulation models, The SABRE Group provided design recommendations that minimized passenger delays and satisfied various performance standards. BAA continues to use the model to assist in the planning and evaluation of alternative terminal designs and operational policies.

Tom sees simulation technology taking on an even more prominent role in the future: "The word is out now that simulation technology is the right way to manage the design of transportation systems. Many of our customers would not even consider making multimillion-dollar decisions without first using simulation. The technology helps to prevent costly mistakes and gives our clients confidence that their implementations will operate smoothly."

▲ Simulation in the Telecommunications Industry

An additional very large and diverse industry that has accepted simulation technology enthusiastically has been telecommunications. Phone companies, internet service providers, and suppliers of computer network architecture are among the many organizations using the tool. In the telecommunications business, organizations are successfully simulating network infrastructure, call centers, maintenance, and other customer-service applications. Simulation allows them to configure information technology and to staff call centers and other customer-service applications appropriately. Areas of focus include the reduction of frustrating customer waiting time and of costly inefficiency in staff schedules. When used for configuring a network infrastructure, simulation technology allows firms to understand the key tradeoff between investment (in hardware and software) and performance (service levels).

SBC Communications Inc.

SBC Communications Inc.

At $23 billion in sales, SBC Communications Inc. is one of the world's leading diversified telecommunications companies and one of the leading wireless communications providers in the United States. Through its subsidiaries, SBC provides innovative telecommunications products and services under the Southwestern Bell, Pacific Bell, Nevada Bell, and Cellular One brands.

Simulation was first introduced at Southwestern Bell in 1994, when Jim Miller, Bob Bushey, and a team of individuals in Southwestern Bell Technology Resources Inc. (TRI), an advanced-technology organization, decided to use the technology to analyze an installation and repair process in Kansas City. The phone company wanted to evaluate various staffing schedules in order to provide the best possible customer service. Senior management was committed to improving the business but wanted proof that increased staffing was necessary. A simulation model helped mid-level management gain approval to hire an additional 50 technicians and dramatically improve service levels.

Soon after the success of the original simulation project, management wanted to consider expanding service to include Saturday installations. An additional model was developed to determine an appropriate staffing schedule that would minimize overtime costs. The change was successfully implemented, and the system performance was very consistent with the model's prediction. From this point, the use of simulation branched into many other areas.

Awareness of simulation's value has spread very quickly throughout the organization. More than 100 SBC sites are now taking advantage of the technology. According to Bob Bushey, "Managers are thrilled with the information provided by our simulation models. They can do a variety of 'what–if' analyses and facilitate very expensive, critical decisions." When asked to point out the most significant benefit SBC has realized through simulation, Bob claims, "Simulation enables our people to gain a far greater understanding of their processes. This argument sells projects to top-level management. Often we find that some of our initial assumptions about our business were not how things really worked in the field. By using simulation, we gain confidence in our decisions."

As simulation spreads throughout SBC, applications are growing and changing. New areas of application include the phone–bill payment center, where tens of millions of dollars in undeposited checks must be expedited. Simulation helps make the system more efficient and profitable.

SBC is also benefiting from simulation as an operational tool for making day-to-day decisions. The same installation-and-repair application that first established the technology within the firm is now being used as a daily scheduling tool. Maintenance-level managers are using simulation to balance their staff schedules each day based on the load of customer orders. Decisions to authorize overtime are very expensive, and simulation reduces the risk of those overtime decisions.

The ultimate goal of TRI is to transfer new technologies to the field operations. This is taking place with simulation. While many of the newcomers to the technology still require some support from TRI, many self-supporting users are arriving on the scene. According to Bob, "Simulation is not only an engineering tool at SBC. Managers use it successfully. Our focus is on business processes. Every manager of a business process should have a model of his process. The future is that for key business processes, you must understand data and you must understand a model. A very strong case can be made for simulation being a requirement for the analysis of all major business processes."

◢ Simulation in the Financial Industry

Banks and other financial institutions, such as credit-card companies, insurance agencies, and mutual-fund providers, are beginning to embrace simulation as well. Among other applications, simulation allows them to analyze the tedious chore of processing checks, insurance applications, credit-card receipts, and various other customer transactions. The key objective in the financial world is to post all customer activities immediately. The difference between a three-day and a one-day delay for posting has significant consequence in terms of cash flow and profit. Simulation allows organizations to identify appropriate resource requirements (e.g., staff, automated equipment) to get the job done on time.

Simulation in Action

ING Group   ING 🦁 BANK

A large user and advocate of simulation technology in this sector is ING Group, one of the world's largest financial conglomerates and holder of various insurance firms. ING Group has its world headquarters in Amsterdam and has offices in many countries throughout the world. Although ING Group is a relative newcomer to simulation, it is quickly spreading its use throughout the organization. The conglomerate's first exposure to simulation occurred when a team of students from the Technical University in Delft (Netherlands) performed a project for Nationale Nederlanden (NN), an insurance company within the ING Group. The project was managed by NN District Director Wim den Ouden. According to Wim, "We were very dissatisfied with our transaction-processing time in one of our post rooms. We decided to simulate the process in order to identify areas for improvement. We were overwhelmed with the project results."

Working with the TU Delft students, NN was able to identify a new methodology that improved transaction processing times by 60%, saving an estimated $1.1 million annually. After the success of this project was touted in an internal company magazine, the acceptance of simulation grew rapidly. Since then, many ING Group employees have been trained in the use of simulation and are now applying the technology successfully. A strategic commitment to the technology for business engineering has been secured at senior levels of management at ING.

According to Wim, "I was initially very impressed by the visualization (animation) offered by the technology. It is a fantastic tool to stimulate people to think of problems and come up with possible solutions. Now, it is the potential for dramatic cost savings and increased competitiveness that makes ING Group and NN very enthusiastic about the technology." Future applications at ING Group include many more transaction-processing projects where the use of automated information technology will be explored to speed up the process. Wim believes that the potential for simulation technology within his organization is tremendous. "We have only just begun to recognize the benefits of this exciting technology. I am confident that ING Bank will dramatically expand our investment in simulation over the next several years."

▲ Professional-Services Firms

Professional-services firms began offering simulation in their consulting practice some time ago. In many cases, they would only use simulation when other analysis methodologies failed them. Today, many of the world's premiere consulting firms view simulation as a powerful way to deliver statistically valid recommendations to their clients—and make a substantial profit in doing so. To the professional-services world, simulation becomes both a powerful problem-solving tool and a differentiating way to sell new concepts and ideas. As briefly discussed in Chapter 3, simulation technology provides an opportunity for professional-services firms to add value to their customer projects.

The fact that simulation has become much easier to use in the last few years has allowed many of the world's leading corporations to invest in and use the technology themselves. At the same time, the use of simulation within the world's leading services firms has also grown at a rapid pace. Often, the services firm introduces the technology to customers, who eventually transfer its use to internal staff. While different industries vary dramatically in terms of their willingness to accept simulation as an in-house tool, they are all reaping the benefit of it—if only via consulting projects.

Simulation in Action

Fluor Daniel   **FLUOR DANIEL CONSULTING**

Fluor Daniel, the principal operating business of the $11 billion parent Fluor Corporation, is the world's largest provider of engineering, construction, and diversified services. Fluor Daniel has been successfully using simulation technology since 1987 for many different client applications. With simulation teams located around the world, Fluor Daniel presents the technology as a value-added service to customers in many industries.

Much of Fluor Daniel's simulation project work facilitates the engineering-design and facilities-improvement projects for which they are well known. However, in other circumstances, they have successfully modeled many service applications and reengineering projects. Fluor Daniel has also completed simulation models for nuclear plant start up and event training, telecommunications network planning and monitoring, and even highway transportation design and analysis. They have also found simulation to be of value for managing internal projects, such as the construction process itself and engineering project management, as part of the company's internal continuous process improvement (CPI) program.

Greg Baker has been managing simulation projects at Fluor Daniel since the company began using the technology. When asked why simulation technology is important to Fluor Daniel and its clients, Greg remarked, "The short answer is that 'good enough' is simply not good enough any more. It used to be that the 'optimal' solution in the real world was always the first one that worked. In today's globally competitive marketplace, this is simply no longer true. Although simulation does not guarantee optimality, it does allow us to approach an ideal system configuration." Greg cites that his clients routinely recognize a 25:1 ROI through Fluor Daniel's simulation applications.

"To our clients, simulation of a new manufacturing process or of upgrades to an existing facility is becoming increasingly important," claims Greg. The two primary reasons for this are limited corporate dollars for facilities upgrades and risk mitigation. In the case of evaluating facility upgrades, simulation allows upper management within Fluor Daniel's client base to evaluate competing expansion projects objectively. Rather than relying on various methodologies for internally selling projects (and competing for limited resources), simulation allows managers to identify clearly which projects are likely to save money and increase profits.

Simulation also helps Fluor Daniel's clients to mitigate the risk involved in dealing with changes in market demand. As the market viability of products and production capacity decreases, a huge variation in consumer wants can bind corporations with inappropriate manufacturing capacities and a noncompetitive market position. According to Greg, "Simulation is often used to mitigate that risk by anticipating great swings in the future production needs and implementing small design changes now, when it is more cost effective."

Perot Systems

perotsystems™

Perot Systems, the $600 million global information-technology services firm, has successfully embraced simulation as a strategic technology and service for the organization and its clients. Perot Systems management considers simulation to be a strategic core competency for the organization. Simulation provides a unique methodology that adds tremendous value to its core IT business offerings by helping clients truly understand the return on investment that any proposed IT solution can deliver.

In the information-technology business—with such application areas as computer hardware configurations, operating systems, networks, databases, call centers, and maintenance—the key variabilities come from manual business processes (that IT investment can replace) and workloads on an automated system (usually spawned by some manual process). "Simulation can visibly, validly qualify and quantify the ROI on IT investments that eliminate or accommodate these business process and system performance variabilities," says Frank Grange, a senior simulation strategist for Perot Systems.

According to Frank, "There is truly no way other than simulation for our external and internal customers to estimate the business value of IT investment. At the rate we are currently demonstrating the value of simulation, we expect that simulation will become part of the company's system/software engineering methodology." Simulation allows Perot Systems' staff to analyze various IT projects, such as understanding the effect of proposed changes—especially IT automation—on improving process throughput. In this case, the financial value of increased throughput can be compared against the investment and incremental operating cost of the proposed change.

In 1996, the simulation staff at Perot Systems grew sixfold. According to Lindy Blackburn, manager of simulation at Perot

Systems, "We expect to at least double in size each year for the foreseeable future. The potential value that simulation offers to clients in the IT business is substantial."

▲ University Acceptance

There are many reasons why simulation is becoming a mainstream problem-solving technology. Easier-to-use software, broad management-level acceptance, and the power of personal computers have all been cited as explanations for the growth in use and awareness that has occurred over the past few years. But perhaps the initial catalyst for simulation technology was university programs throughout the world that began creating a solid foundation of newly trained analysts for the corporate world back in the 1980s. Today, many thousands of individuals graduate from business and engineering schools each year having gained hands-on exposure in the classroom to the technology.

Simulation typically finds its way into the classroom within industrial engineering, operations management, business logistics, and MBA curricula. Other departments, such as computer science, also feature the technology in course offerings. Students generally learn the basics of simulation technology and gain hands-on experience in standard courses. Some students (often in post-graduate programs) will work with local companies to apply the technology to solve real-world problems.

In the United States, simulation is becoming a required part of students' curricula at many universities in departments such as industrial engineering. The Accreditation Board for Engineering and Technology (ABET) works to identify the current set of requirements for industrial engineering and similarly named curricula. ABET requires that students show competence in simulation techniques for an industrial engineering program to be accredited. Initiatives such as these have helped solidify the technology in educational curricula.

Rick Wysk, Leonhard Chair of Engineering at Penn State University, comments that "simulation is the number one method used by industrial engineers to solve problems in industry today." Rick has taught simulation for a dozen years at Virginia Tech, Penn State, and Texas A&M Universities. According to Rick, "Nearly all courses today that deal with manufacturing, production control, and design have incorporated simulation into the program. The technology allows industrial engineers to integrate the many skills they learn in school within a single methodology—one that they will likely use many times as professionals in the business world."

Business schools provide operations management courses that introduce students to the value of simulation. Although the technology is not as integrated in the program as it is in engineering schools, this is changing. Many leading business schools are making the technology a key part of courses on production and business logistics. Some courses provide the opportunity for hands-on experience, while others provide a basic introduction to the technology. In either case, the business managers of tomorrow become acquainted with a technology they can apply to solve real-world problems in the future.

▲ The International Market

The acceptance of simulation outside the United States has in many ways closely mapped its progression in the states. Organizations throughout the world in both the manufacturing and services sectors are reaping benefit from this technology; however, like many technologies that first become accepted in the United States, the acceptance of simulation in international markets has slightly lagged its acceptance in the states.

In Europe, the technology acceptance lag that existed in the 1970s and 1980s has closed in the mid-1990s so that today it is nearly impossible to identify. In fact, according to an informal Gartner Group analysis, "Europeans are more open to the idea of business process modeling than the U.S. market." Several of the industry's leading software and service providers have their headquarters in Europe, and most leading products offer versions in English, German, and other languages.

Some acceptance of simulation in Europe has been driven by U.S. firms who have taken the technology overseas for use in their offshore facilities. For example, in 1989 Compaq Computer—who had been using simulation with success in their Houston headquarters—began simulation project work in their Scotland manufacturing plant. Many other U.S.-based, multinational firms have expanded their use of simulation overseas.

The use of simulation technology within the Pacific Rim continues to lag that in the United States and Europe for several reasons. First, most of the simulation tools in practice today have not been translated to Japanese or Korean language standards. Also, the technology has not yet been endorsed on a wide-scale basis, so many of the new projects must be sold internally to management that is unfamiliar with the tool. However, initiatives such as IMS and the influence of multinational firms are changing this. For example, Honda, Mazda, and Nissan have embraced the technology successfully in the United States, and their experiences are driving an acceptance back at headquarters in Japan.

Other parts of the world, such as South America and the Middle East, vary substantially in terms of their acceptance of simulation. The combination of influence from a strengthening of simulation-technology vendors, multinational firms' acceptance of the tools, and local universities' adopting the technology is driving increased acceptance; however, these markets are mostly at an early stage in the overall adoption of simulation technology.

Simulation Technology—Across the Chasm?

As I stated at the outset of this chapter, simulation technology is emerging as a mainstream problem-solving technology. Evidence I have shared with you strongly suggests that the tool has arrived as a viable one for pragmatic people. At the time of this writing, simulation is at the end of the multiple-decade chasm that has prevented it from appealing to the mainstream user community. Many of the characteristics Moore considers necessary to a mainstream technology (i.e., low price, low risk, etc.) are evident. The market size still indicates, though, that dramatic growth is necessary before we can begin thinking of simulation in the way we now think of CAD technology or spreadsheets.

What is clear is that simulation technology is deeply rooted within some of the world's great companies as an institutionalized methodology for problem solving. Considering the many additional signs of its emergence as an easier-to-use, more widely accepted technique, one must conclude that the technology will play an even more strategic role in the world by the year 2000. A key factor for this technology to continue its momentum into the mainstream is its ability to be positioned as an integrated technology alongside other complementary mainstream technologies. The following chapter will identify "neighboring" technologies to simulation and will articulate the potential leverage that can be gained by marrying simulation with these complementary tools.

5 Competing and Neighboring Technologies

It is not possible to fight beyond your strength, even if you survive.

HOMER

There are many different ways to facilitate change in business. Some decisions are made on the basis of intuition or "gut feel," but most of today's leading companies around the world use a wide variety of computer-based technologies to help them manage large amounts of business information and performance metrics and arrive at important business decisions.

When an organization opts to invest in simulation technology, it is typically buying a tool that will either displace an alternative computer-based method for making decisions or will build on an existing neighboring technology. I will call the alternative method for making similar decisions a *competing* technology. A *neighboring* technology is one that can be leveraged alongside simulation as an integrated solution and business methodology. In this chapter I will explore how other technologies, such as spreadsheets, optimization, scheduling, ERP systems, and business–diagramming software, operate, and I will examine the key issues to consider when adding simulation to your current mix of business engineering software technology.

Several technologies that can be viewed as competing can also be integrated with a simulation strategy. The key is in selecting the best tools for various types of decisions.

I will begin by discussing the software technology that is most prevalent in business analysis today—the spreadsheet.

▲ Spreadsheet Technology

Spreadsheets such as Microsoft® Excel and Lotus 123® offer an outstanding way to store information, understand relationships between variables, and perform complex mathematics in a very easy-to-use format. My life would certainly be much different if I could not rely upon spreadsheets to help in my budgeting and planning activities. I cannot imagine running any significant business without using spreadsheets for analysis and decision making.

It is surprising, however, how heavily corporations rely on spreadsheet technology for making significant, strategic decisions—considering the limitations of this technology. It is not that the mathematical relationships are flawed or inaccurate. Rather, the limitations are in the compromises one must make in terms of describing what is occurring in his or her business.

A simple example will help illustrate this point. It derives from actual experience in the semiconductor industry. Within this industry, spreadsheets have traditionally been used for determining the amount of machine capacity required to manufacture semiconductor wafers. The process of creating patterns on silicon and etching (or inscribing) these patterns requires multimillion-dollar investments for each manufacturing facility. Individual machines generally cost well over $1 million (often as high as $5 million), so determining an appropriate number to get the job done can have a dramatic impact on the profitability of a business.

The application that I became familiar with involved the acquisition of etch machines for a new chip-manufacturing facility. As the company was designing the new facility, a key challenge was to determine an appropriate number of machines to get the job done (i.e., to manufacture semiconductor chips according to forecasted demand). The etch machines carried a price tag of approximately $1.5 million each. A spreadsheet file was used to determine how many should be purchased.

In using the spreadsheet, mathematical formulas were programmed into the individual cells of the file describing the relationships between machines and raw materials. These formulas did a reasonable job of capturing the relationships that exist in the business environment. Ultimately, one spreadsheet cell—after performing many complex calculations—offered a recommendation for the total required capacity. It suggested that eight machines would suffice.

The analysts who were managing this business had been burned before and knew not to trust the static spreadsheet technology. Why? The problem is that the recommendations offered by a spreadsheet file neglect many of the system dynamics that must be captured (i.e., modeled) in order to reflect the reality of a dynamic system. The mathematical equations that form the foundation of the analysis are static in nature. The processing times for resource behavior and the flow of orders through the system are typically basic, static average times. Typically, no variability in performance is taken into account. The result—approximations for resource requirements that are often significantly flawed.

Consequently, the analysts used a "fudge factor" and doubled the recommendation offered by the spreadsheet. The company purchased 16 machines at a total cost of $24 million. When the system was implemented, only 12 machines were actually required to run the business. The company wasted $6 million by overspending for capacity.

Why did these errors occur? First, the spreadsheet-based methodology underestimated the capacity needed because it did not incorporate the system dynamics that must be captured in order to project the future accurately. Second, in the semiconductor business—as in many other industries—it is much worse to have too little capacity than to have too much, so in the face of uncertainty the business analysts overestimated the capacity needed in an effort to ensure that the company would not be starved for capacity.

The system dynamics that spreadsheet technology often fails to capture adequately can be broken down into three fundamental types, involving (1) the randomness and variability in individual process times, (2) the concept of a moving time clock, and (3) the "ripple effect" that many system dependencies have on each other. Simulation technology effectively incorporates all of these dynamics into a business model.

Variability in a semiconductor manufacturing facility exists in many forms. Machines fail unexpectedly. Preventive-maintenance times vary with the skill level of the machine operator and the type of maintenance required. Equipment must be "changed over" and set up again when new products are run through the facility. Also, many individual processes vary each time they are performed. In one week of operation, an individual process may be performed upwards of 3,000 times.

Unless you can describe the true variability in the environment and in each process, you will not be able to "play out" the true behavior of your system accurately. Assuming that each process performs according to an average time will not suffice. You will not get the chance to understand bottlenecks or to see any important system trends—which may include such conditions as starved or overworked resources during certain times of the day.

The concept of the *moving time clock* must now be added to bring your business application to life. When one event occurs, it allows the next event to take place, and so on. When you consider that you may have hundreds of parallel processes taking place simultaneously, you can imagine the impact that time variability may have on your system. As you run a model of a business application for days, weeks, or months of simulated time (in seconds or minutes of computer time), you will gain a realistic perspective of the impact of system variability. Again, a static impression of your business—which often exists in the form of a spreadsheet—does not come close to handling this variability appropriately.

It is also important to understand the *ripple effect* of decision making and interdependence on your application's behavior. Many businesses have a tremendous amount of conditional decision making and general system interdependence that dramatically amplifies the effect of system variability. When you combine the effect of one moving time clock (an event can only begin after the one preceding it has finished) with the fact that many dynamic decisions must be made as the process progresses, you may have a form of chaos in your facility that can produce dramatic swings in your overall performance.

In the semiconductor example, a new order (i.e., a wafer) often requires a specific type of machine for manufacture. For instance, some wafers can only be etched by Machine 1 while others require Machine 2. As the system is operating, these decisions are made dynamically on the shop floor. They also must be captured correctly in the simulation model. The flowchart shown in Figure 5-1 depicts the decision that must be made so that an order can get through the system successfully.

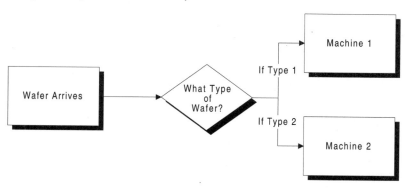

Figure 5-1 *Decision Logic in Semiconductor Example*

As shown, the wafer can go to one of two alternative locations. The decision is made based on the type of wafer being produced. In other situations, decisions are based on basic probabilities (e.g., 30% of the wafers go in one direction, 70% go in another) or various conditional situations. For example, the decision may depend upon the current configuration of the downstream business environment, such as the utilization of specific resources or the number of jobs waiting in queue to be processed by a resource.

Decisions of this sort that are made dynamically in a business will have a dramatic ripple effect on overall business performance measures, such as throughput rates, resource utilizations, and bottleneck behavior.

The combination of system variability, a moving time clock, and dynamic decisions made "on-the-fly" typically is not captured within spreadsheet-based solutions. Simulation technology, however, incorporates all of the required system dynamics into a running model to play out a system's behavior accurately. As we learned in Chapter 1, since there is a significant amount of randomness in a system's behavior, it is important to execute a model many times before drawing a conclusion. If we were to create a simulation model of the semiconductor facility discussed above, the results might look like Table 5-1.

Table 5-1 Summary of Confidence Levels for Making Decision

# of Machines	Confidence Level That There Will Be No Occurrences of Capacity Shortage
11	38.0%
12	78.0%
13	98.0%
14	99.9%

We express a confidence level because we cannot be absolutely certain that any one execution of our dynamic simulation model will be exactly correct. However, we can feel comfortable that we will hit our target performance if we run the model many times and we consistently meet our objective.

In this example, we would likely purchase 13 machines rather than 16. Our tolerance for risk would help us decide between 12 and 13. We would save $4.5 million by using the simulation model for facilitating this decision rather than the static spreadsheet approach.

Even if we could somehow build all of the detailed system dynamics into a spreadsheet file to capture the performance of our business environment accurately, there would still be just cause for using simulation technology instead. One reason is that it is much simpler to create a simulation model than it is to write complex mathematical equations to capture system logic and relationships. For example, in a simulation-software tool, you might express logic in the form of the flow diagram shown in Figure 5-2.

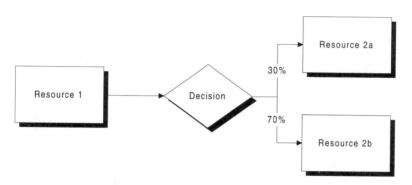

Figure 5-2 *Decision Making with Simulation*

A description of this same decision in a spreadsheet could look like the following:

$$=IF(C9<=0.3,D5,D6)$$

And, of course, this is a very basic example. As the flow diagram and decision-making process become more complicated, the spreadsheet mathematics become more cumbersome. Clearly, the logical placement of graphical objects on a screen to characterize system decision making, order flow, and process times is more intuitive to many than is maintaining complex mathematical formulas to perform the same function.

An additional compelling benefit offered by simulation relative to spreadsheets is animation. As discussed in Chapter 3, animation presents an outstanding vehicle for communicating ideas and understanding your simulated system. When you switch from spreadsheets to graphical simulation, you suddenly migrate from formulas and pie charts to a brilliantly vivid "cartoon" of your business. This cartoon may allow you to make a convincing suggestion to your senior management on a strategic facility-design project.

Without question, business analysts will recognize many benefits when moving from spreadsheet-based to simulation-based planning. However, the use of spreadsheets *integrated with* simulation technology can deliver a powerful combined solution.

Whether or not you rely on spreadsheet technology to facilitate strategic decisions, you most likely at least use spreadsheets as a way to store and manipulate important business information. Thinking in terms of simulation projects, much of the data that must be gathered in order to model your business applications accurately most likely exists today inside a spreadsheet or other database environment. There is no reason that you should have to maintain this information in both technologies. Many simulation products on the market today have some method for directly handing off—or embedding—system data contained in spreadsheets and other databases directly to your simulation model. In this way, you can exploit your existing investment in spreadsheets as data repositories while employing simulation for dynamic modeling.

The benefits of marrying spreadsheets and simulation technology can go beyond simple data exchange. ActiveX™ technologies by Microsoft (formerly known as OLE Automation) can help you integrate many of the best features of the spreadsheet inside a simulation model to perform important functions. For example, Microsoft® Excel offers a "Wizard" for automatically generating charts. This feature can be taken from Excel and used within a simulation tool that supports this technology. Many players in the software industry—vendors of simulation, spreadsheets, and many other tools—are working hard to deliver technologies that can conveniently communicate with other applications. This concept helps end users who wish to combine the best of various tools within a single integrated solution.

▲ Optimization Technology

An additional computer-based technology that is often displaced or augmented by simulation is known as *optimization*. A variety of commercial products on the market allow you to describe your business applications in the form of a series of mathematical functions. Optimization methodologies, such as integer programming (IP), linear programming (LP), and mixed integer programming (MIP), are used by these products to solve problems. Rather than simply executing these programs a single time in order to offer a solution, optimization technology repeatedly "searches" for alternative solutions that are improvements over the one that is currently held as the best. The software program then recommends the best solution that it could come up with. Theoretically, the recommended solution is optimal if all possible alternatives were considered.

If the solution provided by optimization software is truly optimal, why would anyone want to use simulation technology instead? The answer is that the inherent restrictions in optimization algorithms severely limit their application. When they work, they generally work great. Unfortunately, they cannot be used in most applications.

In order to operate, optimization algorithms require strictly defined algebraic equations. In most applications these equations are limited to linear forms with real-valued decision variables. In addition, in most applications the equations define purely static (i.e., no variability) relationships between these variables. Although nonlinear equations, integer variables, and randomness can be accommodated in some special applications, these more flexible representations cannot be applied in general. This is the result of problems in computational speed, as well as the underlying mathematical assumptions (e.g., convexity) that are required to make the methods work. The methods also require a great deal of expertise to apply successfully.

In simulation, we actually "play out" the system operation by moving a time clock forward and updating the system status at each time advance. In this sense, a simulation model is a reenactment of the process that takes place in the real world, and as such it can represent the system in great detail. In contrast, in optimization we solve (either directly or through search techniques) a set of mathematical equations. Although some applications involve time as a variable in these equations, there is no time clock as employed in simulation. In many cases, this severely limits the detail that can be incorporated into the model.

Optimization methods are useful for determining economic order quantity, pricing strategies, and for making various other business decisions. And yet, optimization cannot accurately represent many problems of interest. In contrast, simulation lets us see the future of virtually any complex real-world system by fast-forwarding to tomorrow with an appropriate consideration of all the system variability and interdependence that will occur along the way.

In many business situations, the use of simulation in conjunction with optimization delivers a powerful one-two punch. When using simulation independent from optimization technology, it is sometimes difficult to find enough time to try out all of the possible business scenarios that may be worth evaluating. Simulation analysts are often limited by time (and sometimes patience) when their model is finished, so they evaluate only a small set of alternative hypothetical scenarios. Optimization technology, on the other hand, compromises the dynamics of a business application but does an outstanding job of trying out an appropriate number of system alternatives.

Optimization and simulation technology could be used in a complementary fashion, for example, to design and analyze a supply-chain application or distribution strategy. Suppose that an organization makes shoes at manufacturing facilities and then sends them to central distribution centers. The company wants us to determine an appropriate distribution strategy that will optimize its cost and customer-service performance in transporting its products to the ultimate customers (retailers). Let us assume that we are concerned only with our distribution strategy for the United States. The map in Figure 5-3 depicts our central distribution centers (CDC's) in Las Vegas, Nev., and Memphis, Tenn. Our retailers are scattered throughout the country, but we have identified primary sites (those with the greatest demand). We know that we need to implement a system of regional distribution centers (RDC's) in order to achieve our goals for customer service. However, we are unsure of exactly where the RDC's should be placed in order to optimize our cost and customer-service performance.

Figure 5-3 *Locations of Central Distribution Centers (CDC's)*

Determining where to place our regional distribution centers is a classic optimization problem. As inputs to our optimization program, we would identify such information as distance and cost for transportation. We would also create a series of mathematical relationships that describe the system. For example, one simple mathematical input would be to identify the maximum investment we can make for the new system. This might look like the following:

$$COST < \$50,000,000$$

Another input might be keyed to customer-service-level ratings (CSLR):

CSLR > .95 (in other words, we must hit our customer-service-level target more than 95% of the time)

The optimization software tool may consider thousands of competing configurations for our system. One configuration may have regional distribution centers in Louisville, Atlanta, and Dallas to serve the south and southeast. Another may serve the same retailers from Charlotte and Birmingham. After "searching" for the best configuration—perhaps for hours or even days of computing time—a recommended solution is presented. It might look like Figure 5-4.

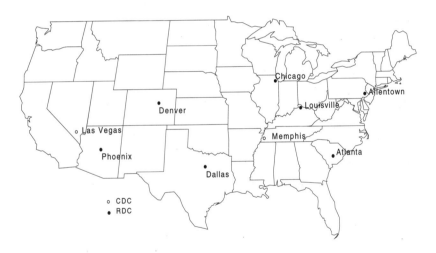

Figure 5-4 *Locations of Central (CDC) and Regional (RDC) Distribution Centers*

The solution provided by optimization technology in this example is likely a good one. However, it is certainly not "optimal." It cannot produce a truly optimal solution, since its assumptions are all based on static information. Dynamic simulation technology would allow us to take this problem a step further.

Much of the system information that was collected to solve the optimization problem is also required for a simulation model of the same application. In making the jump from optimization to simulation, we will initially assume that the recommended solution is acceptable and build a simulation model with these assumptions. In other words, we will accept the fact that our RDC's are in the eight cities identified above. We will also assume that our costs for moving products from one location to the next are accurate and that we have access to the appropriate types of transportation equipment (trucks, trains, planes, etc.).

However, in the simulation application, we must add the variability that plagues any distribution strategy. For example, we must recognize the following variability issues:

▼ Travel times between centers

▼ Truck loading and unloading time

▼ Customer ordering behavior

▼ Manufacturing performance (affecting the supply of products at the distribution centers)

Once we have successfully created a simulation model of this application that appropriately incorporates system variability, we can play out our proposed configuration to see how it will truly perform. We may learn that our customer-service levels will only be met 84% of the time during the critical months of May and June because of the problems we incur in responding to peaks in customer orders. The optimization tool accurately considered that our average service level over the entire year must be 95%. The simulation model allows us to understand how our performance varies over time. The output from our simulation model might look like Table 5-2.

Table 5-2 Customer-Service Levels

	January	February	March	April	May	June
Customer Service Level	0.98	0.98	0.96	0.9	0.84	0.85

Reporting our performance in a time-based fashion is critical to understanding the trends in our system. After all, our customers are very unlikely to complain in the winter when they aren't buying many shoes. It is our performance in May and June that will make the difference between satisfied customers and dissatisfied ones.

In addition to reporting on our customer-service times, the simulation model will help us identify the root of our problem so that we can try alternative scenarios to correct it. In this example, we may have learned that the high seasonal demand creates a bottleneck in our system at our RDC's because we cannot load and unload trucks fast enough. Our simulation output may have included the data shown in Table 5-3.

Table 5-3 Truck Loading Time

	Louisville	Atlanta	Dallas	Chicago	Denver	Phoenix	Allentown
May/June Analysis							
Time to Load Truck (95% confidence)	5.2	9.1	11	6.1	4.8	8	6

This shows that we have a problem in Dallas that needs to be addressed. With our simulation model, we may try a scenario that adds capacity to the Dallas RDC. After we have increased our staff and number of truck docks, we again use the simulation model to understand the impact of this change on our system performance. Obviously, this scenario adds cost to our business; however, it allows us to make minor changes to our overall operation—appropriately taking into consideration the effect of variability—and conduct further cost studies for performance decisions.

Optimization technology can also be used with simulation as a "back-end" tool. If you consider that simulation technology accurately predicts the future for a given hypothetical business scenario but does not "search" for a better solution on its own, the possibility of marrying optimization technology's searching facility with simulation can be attractive. Under this approach, the optimization technology takes the results from a simulation program and attempts to find a better configuration (e.g., increasing the number of resources). After the simulation model is exercised an appropriate number of times for each competing alternative, the optimization product helps to find another viable alternative.

Bringing simulation and optimization technology together in this way is exciting, but it can be tedious. One limitation is that it can take an extremely long time—in terms of computer execution speed—to evaluate appropriately many alternatives in a simulation tool (remember, you need to run models many times before drawing conclusions).

Optimization is not the only technology that enables you to automate the analysis component of simulation project activity. There are other methods—such as design of experiments and goal seeking—that I will not discuss here but that can be easily researched. Simulation vendors are making it much easier to integrate various external tools with simulation software to create automated decision-support environments.

▌ Scheduling Technology

A field closely related to optimization technology is *scheduling*. In fact, many of the scheduling vendors refer to their products as optimization, or at least discuss their methodology for generating an "optimized" schedule. This is because some mathematical system or optimization algorithm for generating a schedule exists inside the scheduling tool. When you "press a magic button," these tools offer a recommended schedule after considering your key performance criteria.

A wide variety of different scheduling tools and methodologies are on the market today. Most medium- to large-sized companies in the civilized world use some form of computer-based scheduling technology. Some of the tools used are sophisticated enterprise-level systems that cost upward of $1 million per plant. Others are more reasonably priced, basic desktop technologies such as Microsoft® Project. And while some companies do not yet use computer-based technology for conducting scheduling, most organizations are beginning to do so, and the market for scheduling software and professional services has grown dramatically as a result.

Scheduling tools are used to generate a specific list of actions that a business must perform to get orders or tasks completed. They generally take into consideration such information as order due dates, order priorities, order routings, and various resource information to generate specific task lists.

While simulation technology is often used in an "offline" mode to evaluate system alternatives hypothetically, scheduling software is generally used as an "online" operational decision-making system that is actually relied upon to manage a facility daily (and in some cases, hourly). Individuals at a facility level, such as shop floor supervisors in manufacturing or staff managers in a credit-card collection department, use the output from scheduling software to sequence orders, schedule agents, and fundamentally run their business.

Output often is presented in a very graphical, easy-to-interpret format called a Gantt chart displaying resources and orders that must be processed, as depicted in Figure 5-5.

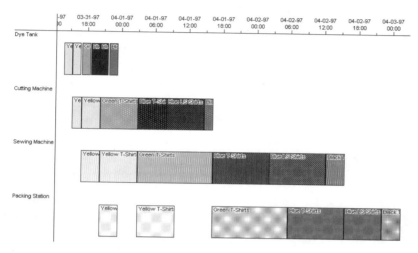

Figure 5-5 *Scheduling-Software Gantt Chart*

Like spreadsheets and optimization technology, scheduling tools make recommendations without regard for system variability. For example, in a manufacturing system, there is a possibility that a machine will break down, preventing orders from being made on time. In a customer-service environment, there is significant variability in the amount of time that a caller could spend on the phone with a customer-service agent. Scheduling software does not account for the variability in these events. Rather, it assumes that resources will be available when orders arrive to them, and it assumes that customer-service "talk times" occur according to an average value. Since the technology maintains a static view of the world, it does not allow you to play out a system to identify bottlenecks. It also does not allow you to gain an appreciation for the effect that the dynamics in your business application will have on your total throughput time, customer-service levels, or utilization of your resources.

119

Do the limitations of scheduling technology make it ineffective? Absolutely not. A key benefit of scheduling software is that it helps you to make a "better" decision than you could possibly have identified on your own—*right now*. While the decision is not truly optimal (since it fails to recognize your system dynamics), it can be a good one. The recommendations made via scheduling software are generally outstanding relative to manual or "back-of-the-envelope" strategies for running a business. Often a tremendous amount of information characterizing your entire business configuration exists within the scheduling product. There is no way that the human mind can handle such a massive amount of information—let alone determine an appropriate schedule for running today's business. And yet, the opportunity to improve dramatically on one's scheduling strategy exists in the form of simulation technology.

Simulation technology allows organizations to "test drive" scheduling strategies prior to implementation. Building a simulation model involves taking many of the same inputs that are fed to a scheduling tool (i.e., resource processing rates, order types) plus the outputs that are generated by scheduling software (i.e., a suggested sequence of events). Once the scheduling tool delivers a hypothesized schedule as an output, a simulation tool provides the opportunity to truly play out this configuration, adequately incorporating the system dynamics into a model.

At a very basic level, simulation technology allows you to build a model of a system—typically using some type of flow-diagram methodology. This flow diagram contains the key resources in your system and presents a process sequence that orders (or phone calls, packages, etc.) must follow. Scheduling technology allows you to input much of the system data—without building a flow-diagram-based model—and returns with a recommended schedule for submitting orders to your facility so they can be processed. The recommended schedule that is output by a scheduling tool is a required input to a simulation application. Once you have input this schedule to the simulation tool, you can "run" the system (and animate it) to understand the effects that system variability presents.

When using simulation, you gain the luxury of working in a hypothetical mode rather than an execution mode. You are able to look ahead to see how your business will perform *before* deciding on an actual implementation strategy. You can conduct "what-if" analysis while appropriately representing system dynamics. As a result, you often make a better, more confident decision with simulation than you could have otherwise.

To illustrate the difference between scheduling technology and simulation, let us again use a simple example. The inputs to a scheduling tool may include those shown in Table 5-4.

Table 5-4 *Inputs for Scheduling Tool*

	Machines	
	Avg. Process Time	**Setup Time**
Machine 1	3	0.4
Machine 2	5	0.8
Machine 3	6	0.9
	Orders	
	Routing Sequence	**# Sold**
Widget 1	1-2-3	25
Widget 2	2-1-3	18
Widget 3	1-3-2	35

Notice that there is no variability in our performance data. Machine processing times and setup times are static (based on an average). No random breakdowns are considered. The concept of time is not an issue here either—it is assumed that all orders exist for this system at the beginning of the day (or at the time when the scheduling program is to be executed). The routing sequence refers to the step-by-step process that each part (i.e., Widget 1, 2, or 3) must follow in order to be made. An additional input not included in the table may be order priorities, so that some consideration is given in the schedule to important customer orders. The scheduling tool utilizes its scheduling algorithm in order to produce a specific recommendation from the static data. The recommendation is presented in a graphical form similar to Figure 5-5.

In order to generate the above schedule, the scheduling software tool executed its algorithm to make all decisions on the sequence in which orders would be released to the system without actually "running" a model forward in time. Unlike simulation technology, where decisions are made "on-the-fly" as a running model performs, scheduling tools typically make all decisions on sequencing and processing of orders at the moment in time when the user opts to generate a schedule.

The inputs to the simulation model would include all of the information contained above on the number of orders, the routing sequence, and any order priorities that may exist. However, we would incorporate the elements of randomness in the model as well. For example, our machine performance times may include the data shown in Table 5-5.

Table 5-5 *Inputs for Simulation Tool*

| | | | Machine Breakdowns | |
| | Processing | Setup | | |
Machines	Time	Time	MTTF*	MTTR**
Machine 1	Min. 1.8	Min. 0.3	Min. 1.8	Min. 0.3
	Avg. 3.0	Avg. 0.4	Avg. 3.0	Avg. 0.4
	Max. 4.3	Max. 0.5	Max. 4.3	Max. 0.5
Machine 2	Min. 3.9	Min. 0.3	Min. 3.9	Min. 0.3
	Avg. 5.0	Avg. 0.4	Avg. 5.0	Avg. 0.4
	Max. 6.0	Max. 0.5	Max. 6.0	Max. 0.5
Machine 3	Min. 4.0	Min. 0.3	Min. 4.0	Min. 0.3
	Avg. 6.0	Avg. 0.4	Avg. 6.0	Avg. 0.4
	Max. 9.0	Max. 0.5	Max. 9.0	Max. 0.5

* MTTF: Mean Time to Failure (time between breakdowns)
** MTTR: Mean Time to Repair (time to repair machine)

You can see that there is substantial variability in the machine process and setup times. Also, machine breakdowns and repair times exhibit randomness—both in their frequency of occurrence (MTTF, or time between breakdowns) and in the amount of time it takes to repair the machines (MTTR). As you run a simulation model of this simple problem for a week of production, you will find that the variability can play havoc with your system.

An additional key input to the simulation model would be a specific schedule and sequence of orders to be released to the system (which were output from the scheduling tool). When working on a strategic project to modify an existing business configuration, you will typically have no opportunity to generate an automatic schedule of a hypothesized system. In this case, you input the anticipated orders and *suggest* a schedule for your model. However, if you are using a scheduling system to automatically generate a recommended facility strategy today as an operational tool, you gain the opportunity to hand this schedule off to simulation technology to evaluate the quality of the schedule. In this case, you are leveraging the strengths of each technology to support business decisions.

▲ Simulation-Based Scheduling

If you study the scheduling-software marketplace today, you will notice that many of the most successful vendors are touting "simulation-based scheduling" solutions. These solutions do not embody the type of dynamic, randomness–enabled, animated technology that has motivated this book. And they are generally not directly integrated with true simulation technology. However, the technology within them exceeds that of a non-simulation-based solution in one specific way.

The one true element of simulation technology (as defined by this book) that simulation-based scheduling tools have captured is the concept of the moving time clock. Unlike traditional scheduling technologies that create an entire facility schedule *now* (without advancing a time clock), simulation-based scheduling technology does consider the fact that as time passes, certain decisions that are made to manufacture a product or handle a customer-service call can affect the overall status of the system so significantly that the key rules for making decisions should be considered *each time* an event must occur. The mathematical scheduling algorithm used by the product executes repeatedly rather than once. The schedule that results is typically of higher quality than is one generated by the non-simulation-based solution.

Simulation-based scheduling systems also differ in that they schedule individual operations during each time advance rather than scheduling an entire job or order at a time. For example, let us assume that the highest-priority order in a manufacturing system requires three operation steps—cut, weld, and finish. The simulation-based scheduling tool would initially schedule the cutting procedure on an appropriate resource. It would then evaluate the initial operations of other orders with high priority and might schedule their first operations before scheduling the welding operation for the first job. This operations sequencing strategy would continue as time progressed, with the simulation-based scheduler creating a schedule that is optimized during each time advance for all orders within a facility. A non-simulation-based tool, on the other hand, would schedule all five operations steps of the first order at one time without regard for other orders that are competing for the same resources. This could lead to a lower-quality schedule.

The simulation-based scheduling solution, however, still lacks the ability to address randomness and variability. Marrying the technology with true simulation in order to evaluate the quality of the recommended schedule again provides a way to create greater confidence in your solution—and most likely, an opportunity to fine-tune the recommendation so that you can achieve better results for your business.

The technologies discussed above—spreadsheets, optimization, scheduling, and simulation-based scheduling—are at times displaced by simulation technology, which offers a more accurate, dynamic methodology for facilitating decisions. In other circumstances, they serve to complement simulation as neighboring technologies in a well-rounded information-technology strategy. The technologies discussed below rarely serve as competing technologies. Rather, they are almost always complementary to simulation.

Business Diagramming

An exciting revolution taking place in the mainstream business engineering marketplace is the widespread acceptance of business-diagramming software tools such as Visio® and FlowCharter®. These products let business analysts easily create flow diagrams and graphic representations of organization charts, network configurations, and many other applications. They deliver the power of basic graphics tools to the everyday user of desktop applications without requiring any specialized skill level. The enthusiasm that exists today for managing information in a purely electronic environment combined with the intuitive nature of business-diagramming software has led to an explosive growth in this market. According to market research conducted by Visio, 60% of all Microsoft Office users (or more than 100 million individuals) desire the type of graphics functionality contained in business-diagramming software.

One popular use of this software is for creating process flow-charts of physical systems. Manufacturing, distribution, customer-service, and many other business process applications are being captured in these tools. Business-diagramming applications often only represent a graphical depiction of a system and do not include specific performance data about how the system operates; however, the tools that exist on the market do have features for adding information to the graphical shapes that symbolize various system components.

The integrated use of business-diagramming technology with simulation is a very natural way for business analysts to engineer a system or process. Arguably, the most natural way for you to describe the sequence of activities in your business application—including the many decisions that occur and interdependencies that exist—is first to create a basic flowchart of the process. You are then in position to "bring the flowchart to life" by adding the various types of information (e.g., resource processing times, frequencies of orders or phone calls, etc.) required to characterize system dynamics.

Many successful users of simulation technology have made a habit of starting every project by initially creating a flow diagram of their business. This approach is a sound one. However, recent developments in the business–diagramming and simulation industries have allowed the two technologies to integrate, so that the flowchart can be converted automatically for use in dynamic simulation. Granted, the flowchart generally does not initially contain all of the information required by a simulation tool, but it serves as a foundation upon which a comprehensive simulation application can be built.

Once it has been converted to a simulation model, the analyst can use animation to "play" the flowchart. Further insight can be gained by viewing orders, jobs, or customer phone calls as they navigate through a flowchart of the business process. For example, by watching the "moving flowchart," the analyst can validate that business decisions are being executed appropriately. He can also more effectively present his business model.

Business-diagramming vendors have made building, modifying, and documenting flowcharts extremely intuitive. In the meantime, simulation vendors have simplified the process of building and using simulation models for managing change. An integrated strategy marries these complementary technologies to gain maximum leverage and reuse of business models.

▲ Computer-Aided Design (CAD) Systems

Over the past 15 years, computer-aided design (CAD) software has become an integral part of how many companies design new facilities. By using tools such as AutoCAD®, designers can create compelling three-dimensional renderings of facilities that incorporate many of the geometric relationships within a computerized layout. It becomes very easy for business users to move equipment, furniture, or conveyors experimentally within a facility by selecting them with a mouse controller and placing them anywhere on the layout. After trying several candidate layout options, the CAD user will select a specific configuration for implementation.

This process of hypothetically moving resources around in a facility sounds very similar to what occurs in simulation studies, no? Of course, the limitation of CAD software—like that of business-diagramming software—is that while it does an outstanding job of capturing the physical reality of a business application, it does not allow you to play out the system in order to understand the performance you will achieve in terms of throughput, bottlenecks, and resource utilization. It contains many spatial relationships but no time-based simulation.

Just as the business-diagramming and simulation-software markets have aligned to allow consumers to leverage the neighboring technologies, so too have the CAD and simulation markets. Many simulation analysts will directly import a CAD drawing into a simulation-software package. Some of the information contained in the CAD system—such as distances and sizes—may be delivered to the simulation model in an automated fashion. Users can apply each technology for what it does best—compelling graphical representations and simulation for accurate process modeling.

◪ Workflow-Management Technology

Widespread interest in office automation and business process reengineering (BPR) have led to the creation of the workflow-management market space. Workflow-management technology has arrived on the scene as a popular yet controversial methodology for facilitating business process redesign. It is used largely by consulting firms as a vehicle for analyzing and implementing fundamental changes to business processes. Implementations typically cut across a large area of a business enterprise. For example, a bank with head-quarters in New York may use workflow-management technology to analyze its customer-service operation across six sites.

While this technology carries great promise and many success stories to date, it is considered high risk by some—for several reasons: the price of required consulting services, the lack of a known market leader (or leaders) for the software, and the lack of standardization on terminology. Organizations such as the Workflow Management Coalition are working to address standards, and the process of free enterprise will likely lead to a smaller number of market-leading software providers.

Like business-diagramming technology, most workflow-management tools (and there are more than 100 commercial alternatives at the time of this writing) employ a flowchart-based methodology for describing the relationships of business processes. Automated business functions—such as database processing, intranet behavior, and electronic document imaging—as well as manual processes are depicted in a graphical manner. The graphical representations capture the flow of "work items" through a customer order-fulfillment cycle.

Workflow-management tools contain details on the routing of tasks throughout a business. A "task list" for each candidate business transaction is provided so that the user can process a task in an automated fashion by using a business model, the task list, and appropriate information (data) for each task.

Workflow-management technology presents a high degree of integration potential with simulation technology. A large amount of the information required to construct an effective simulation model already exists within most workflow-management solutions. In addition to the business flowchart offered by business-diagramming tools, workflow-management applications contain information required to make the flowchart execute. They do not, however, add the element of variability.

By integrating a workflow-management strategy with a simulation strategy, organizations can incorporate the true dynamics of their business within the model. Since most workflow-management projects have the ultimate goal of becoming online operational decision-support and process-control environments, the simulation-enabled model can be extremely valuable for evaluating the proposed "to-be" model without disturbing the actual system. Most workflow-management projects that do not integrate with simulation undergo expensive pilot projects. This is a good approach for all IT initiatives, but cost and time are reduced when simulation is used as a test bed initially.

▲ Enterprise Resources Planning (ERP) Systems

To attempt to fully characterize what are popularly known as ERP systems would be to embark on writing a novel. These tools—sold by companies such as SAP, Baan, PeopleSoft, and Oracle—are far-reaching in terms of their usefulness and need. It is appropriate to discuss them here in terms of the value that an integrated simulation strategy can add.

ERP is the new name for Manufacturing Resource Planning (MRP II). The term was coined by Gartner Group to reflect the fact that MRP II has continued to grow and expand over the years and is really much more today than the old manufacturing-focused name implies.

ERP reaches beyond the plant (the primary focus of MRP II) to include direct communication and coordination with other facilities within the organization as well as with trading partners— both customers and suppliers. ERP also reaches beyond MRP II's traditional functional areas (production, procurement, planning, finance) to presale support (prospect tracking), postsale (field service), quality, and more (Turbide, 1997).

ERP systems are order-transaction systems to run a business and control the flow of finished goods. An ERP system automates and integrates business processes found in manufacturing environments, including those taking place on plant production floors. It has become the means to support and speed the entire order-fulfillment process, including product distribution. By recording transactions (i.e., the computerized records of events such as the receipt of inventory or the issue of a work order), the ERP system tracks resources—such as materials, capacity, and labor—used in financial, manufacturing, and distribution management (Michel, 1997).

As the market emerges, there is a strong trend toward viewing the ERP system as a transaction backbone and data source for integrated decision-support systems. This is where simulation adds value to ERP implementations.

One way that simulation complements ERP is in providing "look-ahead" capabilities to support decisions prior to implementation. Rather than always relying on the execution of ERP for carrying out tasks, an analyst using simulation can explore alternatives before processing a decision (or series of transactions) via ERP. When simulation is integrated directly with ERP technology, this look-ahead functionality can be housed within the ERP software environment, so that decisions made after conducting "what-if" analysis are automatically entered in the ERP product. In this case, ERP serves as the foundation or backbone for business management. The simulation tool serves to facilitate potential changes to the default way of thinking that lives within the ERP system. These changes are evaluated with appropriate regard for system variability and can be displayed in a compelling fashion with dynamic animation.

Simulation can also complement an ERP implementation strategy when the technology is used prior to determining an appropriate business model from which the ERP system will be structured. In this case, simulation technology identifies the best "to-be" business scenario from a cast of many options. Since all ERP systems require some type of business model (largely characterized by a proprietary database architecture) that captures the many relationships that enterprise processes have to each other, the ultimate "to-be" business model that a successful simulation study produces can be directly leveraged when implementing ERP.

Although they somewhat overlap ERP in terms of their problem-solving domain, workflow-management systems are focused on business process paths such as credit or engineering approval, document imaging, or intranet, whereas ERP aims at the specific manufacturing fulfillment events that must take place to satisfy customer orders. Integration of ERP and workflow-management technology—for example, embedding a workflow-management solution within an ERP solution so that customer orders can be routed automatically to the appropriate business paths, such as to receive credit or engineering approval—presents an even stronger enterprise solution.

Many other information-technology solutions may be leveraged as part of a successful simulation strategy. As many leading software vendors continue to focus on "open," easily integrated component-based software, the likelihood that you will be able to leverage your entire information-technology investment across many application areas grows each year.

6 A Strategy for Implementing Simulation

What is the first duty—and continuing responsibility—of the business manager? To strive for the best possible economic results from the resources currently employed or available.

PETER F. DRUCKER

Like any sophisticated computer-based problem-solving technology, simulation used wisely can reap significant reward—and misused can lead to disappointment. Professionals in the simulation-software industry have worked hard over the past 10 years to simplify the process of developing models. Consultants and professors have endorsed various methodologies for applying simulation technology. Some offer a "cookbook" approach (for example, one consultant offers a 14-step remedy for successful application of simulation, while others have simplified the process into as few as five steps).

The first issue in wise use of simulation technology within your firm, though, is not "how" but "when": *"When should you make the move to invest in simulation?"* Accordingly, this chapter first addresses the *timing* of your decision to begin using simulation. It also addresses various organizational issues that you might consider before actually launching a simulation effort.

Strange as it may sound, you actually have somewhat of an advantage if you haven't already started a simulation strategy within your organization or department. This is not because the technology just recently appeared on the scene. Rather, it is because the tools have improved so dramatically that your probability of success with a single project is much higher today than it was in the past. The likelihood that you will be able to propagate the use of simulation successfully throughout your enterprise has grown as well. However, you should not wait much longer to begin, because other firms in your business that are already exploiting this valuable technology may put you at a competitive disadvantage.

As is often the case when utilizing technologies that carry a promise of substantial savings, it is important that your early experiences be successful and far reaching in terms of their effect on your business and their visibility within the organization. I have watched many companies begin to use simulation, and there is often a pattern of behavior and expectations. Here is what often occurs:

▼ There is a tremendous amount of excitement for the technology when it is initially purchased.

▼ Individuals involved in the process may not truly understand the technology—especially management.

▼ During the initial project, several other projects are identified immediately. The promise of simulation becomes known, and many individuals "jump on the bandwagon."

▼ One person leads the simulation effort as the internal "champion" for the new technology. He or she is the only person trained in the use of the tool.

The first project may be wildly successful, saving the company considerably more than was invested in software, support services, and time. Or, owing to one of a number of potential problems, the project could fail miserably. The point being made here—and it generally applies with the introduction of new information technology—is that early experiences often lay the groundwork for making simulation either a standardized methodology for business problem solving or a technology that is applied only in special-case situations—if at all.

134

In light of the foregoing, let us examine a few key questions:

▼ When is the "right" time to invest in simulation technology?

▼ What should you do after you have made the decision to invest in simulation?

▼ How should you manage successful simulation projects?

▼ How can you distribute the use of simulation throughout your enterprise?

■▲ When Is the "Right" Time to Invest in Simulation Technology?

Unlike first aid, simulation has a right time for its introduction. The key is to introduce it when you can leverage various organizational factors that will allow you to grow the use of simulation as a significant problem-solving tool for your firm.

First, since simulation technology is a powerful way to facilitate change, you need to make certain that you have a significant change to facilitate. Sounds basic, doesn't it? For example, I would be more inclined to introduce simulation as a way to perform a significant upgrade to a facility, to support a facility consolidation, or to help design an entirely new business operation than to buy it simply to capture today's business configuration in a model for future reference. I have often experienced situations where an organization invested in simulation simply because they felt that they needed to do so (perhaps a manager saw the technology at another firm and mandated the technology). No consideration was given to identify a specific objective for the project or a specific change that could be facilitated. In this case, the opportunity to position the technology within the firm was lost and the likelihood of success was compromised.

A good opportunity to introduce the technology is to improve a system that is operating poorly in terms of customer-service performance or in terms of excess inventory carrying cost. Look for an existing system that you are confident can be improved by analyzing other alternatives. In this case, you may not have a corporate strategy to upgrade the facility or dramatically change it, but you know that you can manage your current resources more effectively by designing a better system for managing orders or customers.

The key is to look for high-impact projects that will allow you to demonstrate the value that simulation technology contributed. You should try to achieve at least enough ROI on your initial project to cover your investment in software, support, and time. If you do this—and there is no reason why you should not—you will quickly gain the corporate buy-in that you desire to advance your simulation efforts. Plus, you gain the opportunity to leverage simulation technology for consistent cost savings for your firm, and you gain the opportunity to achieve the career growth that you seek.

The impact of your first project does not have to be facilitywide. It could focus on a single costly bottleneck problem that is critical to your business, or it might examine various material handling strategies for operating one specific area of a warehouse. Start small and show results quickly! You want to facilitate an improvement that has some meaningful level of cost, aggravation factor, and organizational visibility.

Beginning with a small project allows you to pilot the new technology and quickly advance on the technology learning curve, so that you are in a position to grow your capability quickly. If you are faced with a large facility-level or enterprise-level (e.g., supply-chain) project, you may want to outsource at least the first project. You should not be intimidated by the large project (since it may offer a tremendous opportunity to achieve substantial payback for your efforts and high corporate visibility). Just make certain that you are equipped to handle the effort, because your project will likely be closely watched by senior management, and your performance could affect the place of simulation technology (and your career) within your firm.

The issue of whether you perform the project as an in-house activity (by your own employees) or hire it out to a professional consulting firm should be made on the basis of your resource availability and time. Clearly, it behooves you eventually to develop some level of simulation talent within your firm so that you can maximize the return on your investment in projects; however, you should also recognize that timing is very important and that—in spite of tremendous advances in software ease of use—the application of simulation technology comes with a learning curve. Make sure that you seize the opportunity to save your company money and avoid risk when you can—even if it means relying on outside talent to manage your initial project.

Many companies making the decision to conduct simulation in-house opt to hire an outside consultant for a few days of assistance during their initial project. A consultant highly skilled in the use of simulation can help you fast-track your first project to increase its likelihood of success. This approach will also help your people accelerate their learning of the tool and project methodology.

No matter how you introduce simulation to your organization, you will want to invest in some level of education. Educational manuals and/or courses are readily available from software vendors, consultants, universities, and various other sources. The World Wide Web is packed with simulation sites containing useful information on the technology, its value, and how it should be applied.

Knowing that you can expedite a significant change may prompt you to introduce simulation within your firm. Before proceeding, however, you should confirm your company's willingness to accept the results of your project. Make certain that your project has management's attention. You will need this in order to convert your recommendations into actions. I have seen effectively run projects produce little or no change because they did not have the appropriate level of management participation. This subject will be addressed again later in this chapter.

What Should You Do After You Have Made the
▲ Decision to Invest in Simulation?

Let's assume that you have effectively reviewed your company's business environment. You know that a visible, high-impact change needs to be facilitated appropriately. You are confident you can achieve the level of management participation that you require. Now what do you do?

Let's start with your objectives for the project. I would suggest that they are something like this:

▼ You want to save money for your company.

▼ You want to select the "best" way possible to manage your business.

▼ You want to gain approval from management so that recommendations can be implemented.

▼ You want to expose your firm to a new technology that can deliver repeated value to projects.

Achieving these objectives is not that difficult—just so long as you position yourself for success. Your first step is to "frame" the problem and possible solution. This should take the form of a basic project statement—preferably one that fits on a single page. Consider the following example:

> Our business performance has been outstanding. Orders are increasing and growth is strong. As stated by our division vice president, we must undergo a 75% increase in the capacity of our current warehouse by next spring. This objective must be met to handle our anticipated forecast. If we do not achieve this target, we stand the risk of paying exorbitant fees to outsource some of our storage requirements.

> Additionally, we are concerned about the current warehouse configuration that is struggling to maintain our stated customer-service goals. Our average order-fulfillment time is 15% slower than our stated service target. This problem must be addressed immediately or we will begin suffering the consequence of losing valuable customers.

To address these two challenges, we will utilize simulation technology. Our initial effort (Phase 1) will focus on the immediate-term challenge of improving customer-service performance in our existing warehouse. Shortly after completing this effort, we will begin evaluating expansion strategies (Phase 2), so that we can identify the most cost-effective warehouse configuration to meet the objectives established by our division vice president.

During Phase 1, we will model our order picking and retrieval process so that we can identify the right mix of staff and material handling equipment to achieve our target service goals for our current operation. Simulation technology will first allow us to identify the best configuration, given our current resource commitments. If we determine that additional resources are necessary to achieve our service targets, we will be able to identify the minimum required investment to meet our goals.

After successfully applying simulation to improve the performance of our existing operation, our Phase 2 effort will focus on the development of various candidate warehouse configurations so that we can optimize our investment in resources and be prepared for our upcoming expansion. Our objective is to make certain that our anticipated increase in facilities investment is minimized while giving us a high degree of confidence that our future performance goals will be met.

Our project timetable is shown in the accompanying figure.

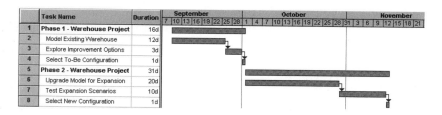

Figure 6-1 *Warehouse Improvement Project*

This statement clearly identifies why simulation will be used, states objectives for the study, and presents a timetable for successful project completion. This document serves as the foundation upon which the entire project will be managed.

As a strategy for effective project management, the project statement above has been broken into two distinct phases. The first phase involves improvements to your existing operation, and the follow-on phase focuses on the significant facility expansion. Although you may not have the luxury of starting with a pilot project, one that is somewhat smaller than your ultimate project, I suggest that you do so, if possible. The improvements to the existing application in this case will be the pilot. Again, you want the first initiative to have high visibility, but you are also looking for a quick success. A smaller application gives you the opportunity to show results immediately and helps you generate increased enthusiasm (and confidence) for making the jump to a larger, more strategic application.

After you have framed the project, you should identify potential areas for savings. It is always wise to project a positive ROI at the outset, so that you can articulate the potential savings that the project may deliver. As your project concludes, this ROI projection will help you evaluate your bottom-line performance relative to your expectations. You might cite the following potential savings for your warehouse simulation project:

▼ Phase 1 (upgrade to existing system):

    ◆ Our simulation project will allow us to improve our current warehouse operation by considering various alternatives for order picking and material handling. We expect to decrease our average response time for satisfying customer orders by at least 10%. We also intend to identify better ways to utilize our resources (i.e., people, fork trucks). This will allow us to eliminate unnecessary equipment. It is our expectation that we will save at least $100,000 in unnecessary investments in capital while gaining substantial improvements in customer service.

▼ Phase 2 (facility expansion):

    ◆ It is imperative that we purchase the right amount of conveyor capacity for our new warehouse expansion project. Each section of conveyor rack costs $85,000. The simulation model will help us identify the best configuration. Based on our past performance of overspending for capacity, we are likely to save at least $500,000 by purchasing the right amount of conveyor capacity.

- Outsourcing costs $30 per square foot of storage space. It also creates an inconvenience in terms of satisfying customer orders in a timely fashion. By using simulation to size our new facility effectively, we will not incur any outsourcing fees. Based on previous experience, this will likely represent a savings of $200,000 per month for the first four months of operation.

- As we expand our business, it is also critical to deliver exceptional customer service. By using simulation, we will gain confidence that our proposed facility will achieve our targeted level of customer service.

In addition to identifying possible areas for savings, you should always commit—to yourself and to your management—that you will save more than you will spend on the project. This is a simple idea, but the point is that it is not enough to communicate potential savings. You need to commit firmly to realizing some level of quantified savings. My advice is to undercommit so that you can overdeliver. The commitment you make must be enough to generate enthusiasm (and establish a sound business case), but you should plan to do much better.

As stated in Chapter 3, there are many "softer" benefits of simulation that are difficult or impossible to quantify. It is always worth mentioning some of these—such as the fact that you are gaining a type of insurance policy by simulating a strategic facility change prior to making it. You are helping to avoid the risk of implementing a system that may not deliver enough conveyor or floor-space capacity. And, you might point out that having an animated simulation model of your proposed warehouse will help communicate project ideas to management and help train individuals on the warehouse floor in the implementation phase of the project. I suggest, though, that you always lead with some form of projected ROI and consider the softer benefits to be luxury items.

Your next step is to make sure that you are communicating with your senior management effectively. You should fully explain your aspirations for a successful project and—at the same time—give them an opportunity to impact the direction of your study. By communicating effectively early in the project, you can win the management "buy-in" that you seek. You may also learn more about specific goals that your management has for the expansion project, so that you can account for them in your study.

When you meet with your management to share your understanding of the project's business objectives, goals, and potential cost savings, you should also have a prepared summary of the individuals you will need on your project team. Ask your management, too, to publicize the importance of the simulation study throughout your department. This will help you gain the level of participation you will need from those you will count on for detailed information.

If you effectively manage your simulation projects, the technology can become a vehicle around which many individuals within your organization rally to make decisions. For example, in the warehouse example, you may have involvement from the vice president of distribution, the facility manager, your three-person engineering staff, and various individuals who work on the warehouse floor. Each is important for particular reasons.

The vice president may make the ultimate decision on any capital investments that your project would suggest. The facility manager may be the authority on facility layout decisions. Your three-person engineering team must communicate fluently, so that you can all affect the various layout and resource scenarios that you will want to evaluate. One of your engineers may be working on CAD (computer-aided design) facility layouts that you will use for the animation of your model. Another engineer may be responsible for making certain that all facility information is available in convenient database formats for the project. Perhaps you are the one who is implementing the actual simulation tool. Individuals on the warehouse floor are required to validate all of the decisions that are made in storing and retrieving orders. They will provide detailed information on activities that your simulation model will capture. If you do not already have quality data on the way your business behaves, these people may be needed to help you capture this information for the first time. Although you may be doing most of the project work yourself, it is worth having on-board, at the onset of your simulation effort, everyone on whom you will rely to provide some level of support.

In summary, you want to make sure that you get off to an outstanding start on your simulation project by stating your specific project objectives—including ROI projections when possible—communicating with management, and securing an appropriate project team to ensure a successful initiative. Once you have done this effectively, you are ready to execute on a high-impact simulation project.

How Should You Manage Successful Simulation Projects?

You were successful in first convincing yourself and then your management to make simulation the technology that will help your company manage change. Now it is time to direct the project successfully so that you can deliver—better yet, exceed—what you promised.

You identified specific project objectives in communicating the project internally. Now, you need to convert these objectives into questions that the simulation model will help you answer. For example, we stated earlier that an objective for Phase 1 of our project was to decrease our average response time for satisfying customer orders by at least 10%. The questions may be posed as follows:

▼ What mix of staff and material handling equipment will generate a 10% improvement in customer-service times?

▼ What layout changes would improve customer-service times?

▼ What changes to our order-picking sequence would improve customer-service times? Should we fill multiple orders concurrently or focus on high-priority orders first?

At the most fundamental level, simulation allows you to answer questions that you may not have been able to address otherwise. As a project manager, you are more concerned with getting valuable answers to difficult questions than you are in creating an elegant model of your business. If you begin by first crafting the critical questions you have for your business, you will help to make certain that you manage your simulation project in a highly focused manner.

As in any important business undertaking, you should maintain a strict schedule for successful completion of your project. I suggest that you publicize the project schedule to everyone involved. If your project is a two-week simulation effort to analyze a small portion of your business application, you may simply communicate the project schedule via a project kick-off meeting. On the other hand, if you are performing a more significant, lengthy effort, I suggest that you post the project schedule in a conference room or "project war room" for everyone to see. As you accomplish specific project milestones, you can mark your schedule board appropriately. Managing your project aggressively according to a well-thought-out schedule will help everyone stay on pace for a successful project completion. Figure 6-2 shows a possible schedule for Phase 1 of the warehouse improvement project.

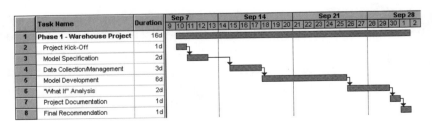

Figure 6-2 *Simulation Project Timetable*

▲ Project Kick-Off

Invite everyone on your simulation project team to your project launch meeting. Ask your vice president to make a few statements about the significance of the project. During the meeting, summarize the key project objectives and the key questions you expect to be answered. Identify specific roles that individuals will play, and carefully review your project timeline. You should also take this opportunity to identify the types of data that you require. You may need to modify your project schedule if you find that certain types of information are not readily available.

If you have your act together going into the project kick-off meeting, you will likely have an easy time achieving success. There is a tremendous benefit in spending a little extra time in preparing for the kick-off, since it helps you communicate the importance of the project and gain appropriate buy-in from individuals who will ultimately participate. If you fail to organize a meeting of this type, probably you will be forced to meet with each of the same individuals anyway, but you will have failed to establish the effort as a teamed project from the onset and to establish its significance via the participation of your vice president. The information you need to get the project done on time may now be much more difficult to generate. So—a little salesmanship and project management leadership up front will go a long way in making your project a success.

If you feel it is appropriate, you may even hold a second meeting for a broader, facility-level audience to alert them to what is going on. This may shift them over to participate eagerly in the project rather than fearing it. You should also make certain that you meet as a team on a regular basis as the project progresses in order to monitor and/or revise your schedule.

▲ Model Specification

The project schedule is an important tool for managing and monitoring the progress of your project. It should be complemented by a *model specification*. This document identifies the following:

▼ *The application you are simulating.* Identify the scope of your project in terms of size (e.g., entire facility or one small area) and activities within it. Identify the way decisions are made in the system. For example, state how the current warehouse operates in terms of its order-picking strategy: When do workers get orders? Do they use pallets? What happens when a bar-coding machine breaks down? Graphical flowcharts can help communicate decision-making procedures effectively.

▼ *The required data inputs to the model.* Information such as an order forecast, travel times for fork trucks, distances between workstations, and picking times should be listed as necessary information for creating a model. By listing your data requirements, you will be able to identify quickly what you have and what you need to collect. You should also identify the format of the information (e.g., spreadsheets or databases).

▼ *The types of analyses you intend to perform.* Identify the key variables in your application and how you will conduct "what-if" analysis. In your warehouse, for example, you may be able to vary the number of workers, the number of fork trucks, and certain aspects of your layout. If there are limits on the amount of change you can explore (e.g., you may not have the luxury of increasing the number of fork trucks), you should state this. By identifying the types of business scenarios with which you can experiment, you will help focus your model development and expedite your "what-if" scenarios when your model is complete.

▼ *The types of information you intend to report.* Your final decisions will be based on information generated by your simulation model. If you are concerned about customer responsiveness, make sure that you are reporting on the time it takes from the moment your customer places an order to when the product has been retrieved. It is also likely that you will want to know how busy your resources are in terms of their percentage utilization. If you do, say so in this portion of your model specification.

At this point, you will have documented the following key project components:

- ▼ Project objectives (stated when framing the problem)
- ▼ Project schedule
- ▼ Model specification

These three items should be easily accessible by everyone involved in the simulation effort. My advice is to go through a very brief validation step (this may entail a lunch meeting with your division vice president) to make certain you are on track before moving to the data-management phase. Share your documentation with the appropriate individual(s) to check your understanding of the project. You may find that you do not need to model a certain area of the warehouse or that an additional project goal should be added. Consistent checking of your project plan against your business goals is a smart strategy for staying on target and maximizing the return on your simulation initiative.

▲ Data Management

The old "garbage-in, garbage-out" theory holds true for simulation projects just as it does for many other IT initiatives. Solutions are only as good as the underlying data and assumptions allow them to be. The key is to effectively identify the information you need for the project in your model-specification phase so that you can focus on getting this information in the data-management phase.

If you are moving from an "as-is" to a "to-be" configuration, you will need to begin with data that characterizes today's system. Since you are trying to incorporate the true variability of your business into a simulation model, you must have enough historical data values in order to make an accurate assessment of how specific processes take place. In some cases, you may find that you need to invest in the time and resources to collect data manually in your business environment. In others, you should be able to access historical system performance contained within a database or spreadsheet system.

When modeling an entirely new operation, you often use a combination of historical performance from similar facilities, rough estimates, and, at times, industry standards. Often you can get information on machine performance from the vendor. Information on the frequency of breakdowns and expected time to repair, for example, can be ascertained without relying on historical research.

Collect as much information up front as you possibly can. If you are modeling a small area of a facility, this information may be readily available. Larger projects and new-facility projects present a greater challenge. Do not let yourself become a victim of a stalled project that is waiting for valid system data. As stated before, if you do an effective job of communicating your project requirements early in the planning process, you will be less likely to encounter significant problems during the data-management phase.

Sometimes even effective communication is not enough. Individuals who commit to providing information early in the project may get distracted and fail to deliver on their commitments. Since you cannot complete an effective simulation model without valid system data, you may be forced to make estimates or assumptions that compromise the accuracy of your model output. If all else fails, you may need to seek a higher authority (perhaps your enthusiastic division vice president) to aid in prioritizing data management for others on your simulation project team.

Of the many simulation projects I have observed, data management more often wreaks havoc on successful simulation initiatives than any other project component. I strongly encourage you to do your homework up front (via effective communication and management participation) to lay the groundwork for a flawless project experience.

▲ Model Development

Many newcomers to simulation assume that the bulk of the project effort is dedicated to model creation. This, quite simply, is not the truth. This misperception may arise because simulation-software vendors emphasize model development rather than successful simulation project management, implying that the focus of any project is the model itself.

It is estimated that on average, simulation analysts devote about one-third of their overall project time to model formulation. If the necessary model data has been collected appropriately and if the software tool being used is straightforward, model development should not be a problem. The model-development methodology utilized by various simulation products differs in terms of features and product terminology; however, at a basic level, you construct a logical system that describes process flow (perhaps using a flowcharting tool), add system data, and create an accompanying animation.

When your simulation project is aimed at improving upon an existing system, a key component of the model-development phase is a careful validation of the model against the actual system. When modeling an "as-is" operation, the business analyst should first create a model that mimics the actual system's performance. Rather than running the model with time variability, the model should be executed with recent historical data (if it is available) so that the actual system performance can be reproduced. If detailed historical data is not available for certain operations—such as a manual picking station in the warehouse—random distributions may be used for validation; however, the most accurate validation occurs when actual data are used. Only after the model has been proven to be accurate should various "to-be" alternatives be tested and time variability introduced. (Remember, we introduce time variability to predict the future based on our past experience.)

If your simulation effort addresses an entirely new system, you should validate your model against the rules and information contained in your model specification. In this case, you are checking to make certain that you have correctly captured the system logic that your candidate "to-be" system would utilize. You should also use some general intuition and application experience to evaluate carefully the results that your model is producing to make certain that they seem to be appropriate for your proposed business. If you are modeling a large facility, it is wise to validate small areas individually so that you can increase your confidence level that the aggregate system will be modeled correctly.

Animation can play an invaluable role in successful model development and validation. First, it provides an easy-to-understand environment for graphically constructing a model (that is, if you are using a simulation tool that integrates animation with simulation); and next, the use of animation simplifies the process of validating your model against either the actual system or the model specification. Rather than trying to interpret model logic or simulation output, you simply sit back and watch a dynamic cartoon of your facility operate before your eyes.

▲ "What-If" Analysis

After a validated model has been developed of a system under review, it is time to test the model under a wide variety of alternative conditions. For example, it may be appropriate to evaluate various competing resource configurations. One scenario may have six machines and six staff. Another may have nine machines and three staff, and so on. Each scenario of significance must be run many times or for a lengthy duration so that the effects of randomness are appropriately played out (i.e., you should never make a decision on the basis of a single run or an abbreviated run, since you will not have statistically valid information).

Simulation analysts often do not allow for enough analysis time. It is not uncommon for a simulation project to be stalled briefly by a lack of data, which may throw the project off schedule. Inevitably, the aspect of the project that gets compromised is analysis. After the model is completed, there may be only a day—or perhaps a few hours—before the presentation of your results and recommendations to management, so you scramble to finish at least a small percentage of the overall analysis that you had intended to perform.

Some simulation products provide features that allow you to automate some of your analysis. For example, you may be able to automatically try out 15 different resource-configuration scenarios by simply identifying possible ranges (minimums and maximums). This technology can expedite the "what-if" analysis phase considerably, allowing you to focus on considering the pro's and con's of your finalist alternatives rather than on the mechanics of changing and running the model repeatedly.

Remember, when you are using simulation, you are trying to achieve an outcome that is the best you can possibly identify. Your outcome may not be theoretically optimal, but it should be as good as you can make it. The more time you spend exploring system alternatives, the more likely it becomes that your final solution is nearing optimal.

The transition from model development to system analysis often occurs several times during a successful simulation project. You may find as you try various business scenarios that you actually want to change the model itself rather than simply manipulating data values. One or more of your scenarios may involve unique system logic that generally requires a change to the model. You may ultimately select a configuration that has the best combination of process flow and resources. This methodology may force you back and forth between model development and analysis.

▲ Final Project Documentation

Another phase of successful simulation projects that is often overlooked or at least compromised in terms of quality is the final project documentation phase. If you are modeling an application that is occurring simply to support a single decision, where you are the only person involved with the project and where you fully expect never to use the simulation model after the decision is made, then you may not need to worry about documentation. Chances are, however, that you want to use the model beyond an initial decision, that you intend to share it with others, and that you plan to grow your application as the system grows. In this case, you should wrap up a successful simulation project with a project documentation phase.

The project steps you are now documenting should be a natural extension of the earlier documented steps (i.e., project objectives, project schedule, and model specification). You can take the previous items as inputs to the final project documentation process. You basically add additional project information to what you already have in order to complete your summary of the effort.

In the final project documentation phase, you should summarize any key characteristics of the model that you created, such as your approach for sharing resource groups and the way you prioritized certain customer orders. Any complex system rules that you may have captured in the model should also be stated (hopefully, these rules already exist in your model specification), and you should identify the types and sources of data that you used for the project. You should also take the time to summarize the key findings of your simulation project. What insight did you gain from the study? What business scenarios did you chose not to recommend? What were the benefits of the ultimate "to-be" scenario versus others?

There are many reasons why you should spend an additional few hours near the end of a simulation project to complete useful documentation that can be referred to in the future. In addition to the obvious benefit of making it easier for you and/or someone else to return to the project in the future, quality model documentation can help to sell simulation internally (i.e., "look what we did with simulation"), and it may help your firm establish a standardized methodology for effectively using simulation.

While I refer to this documentation phase as something that occurs near the end of a successful simulation effort, clearly documentation should span the entire initiative. Consistent use of documentation—and consistent communication—throughout a project can help to involve key personnel at intermediate points, and it demonstrates to your organization that simulation projects are methodologically sound and serious—unlike, for example, the ad hoc use of spreadsheets for problem solving.

▲ Final Recommendations

The use of simulation—especially when accompanied by an impressive animation—provides a very compelling way for you to sell project ideas and recommendations to senior management. You should take advantage of the opportunity to illustrate the best way for your business application to be implemented and managed.

Whenever possible, be sure to articulate the quantified savings that one implementation strategy may have over another. Your arguments will generate much more impact if you state savings and quantified improvements as part of your final report or final presentation. You should share information on the methodology that you utilized, including a synopsis of the various alternatives that your project team explored, stating your rationale for making the final recommendation.

Remember also that, in delivering your final recommendation to management, you have an outstanding opportunity to position simulation as a critical technology for future projects. You might suggest other applications for the tool as you are sharing the final results of your initial project. This gives you a chance to build momentum for the new technology in the mind of your senior management, so that you can expand the return on your investment in simulation across the enterprise.

▬ How Can You Distribute the Use of Simulation
▲ Throughout Your Enterprise?

There is no reason why you should not be able to exploit the value of simulation routinely throughout your company. The amount of internal selling and coaching required for each subsequent simulation project should decrease as your company migrates from its early experiences with simulation to widespread use. However, getting from early acceptance to enterprisewide use requires the right mix of success, enthusiasm, and momentum.

Because simulation is often viewed at first as an "elective expense" (one that is not absolutely necessary in order to design a facility or upgrade an existing one), it must be justified internally on the basis of offering a good chance to save the company more money than it will cost. Its elective-expense status stems largely from the fact that many managers simply are not aware of what the technology is and how it works. The key for you as an enthusiastic supporter of simulation technology is to recognize that management often has this view by default, so that you take appropriate action to educate them on its potential value.

Eventually, you will need to change management's perspective of simulation so that it becomes an accepted way of managing your business. You want to get to the point where you are integrating simulation into your business methodology: Simulate first, build second. Simulate first, upgrade second. Given the extremely high investments in capital, people, and inventory made by firms today, it is easy to see the role of simulation in managing change.

There are several effective strategies for rapidly spreading the use of simulation throughout an enterprise. In order to understand better how they work, let us examine briefly two contrasting business models for how decision-support and business-management software like simulation are managed throughout an enterprise.

▲ "Push" versus "Pull" Business Models

Organizations today vary dramatically in terms of their organizational structures. The reengineering craze of the mid 1990s created a tremendous number of team-based organizations, in which decision authority has moved from a central site to field locations (a.k.a. "empowerment"); however, very traditional configurations continue to exist. Most companies offer some combination of teams as well as some traditionally organized functional departments. Regardless of the firm's specific organizational structure, there is typically some concept of corporate-level support and facility-level support for information technologies. Figure 6-3 oversimplifies the idea to help support a point.

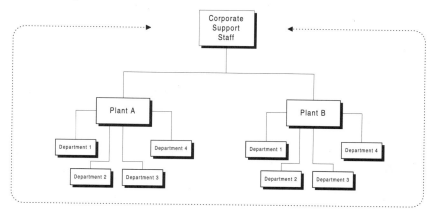

Figure 6-3 *Example Organizational Structure*

A "push" business model can be defined as one where corporate staff has a significant impact on the acceptance of information technology throughout an enterprise. The corporate staff—often located at a world headquarters facility—generally take the initiative to evaluate new technologies for introduction within the firm. This does not imply that the facility-level sites do not have the expertise to utilize information technology—rather, the organizational culture is such that most new technology decisions of any consequence (perhaps those over a specific dollar amount) must be directed by a corporate function.

A "pull" business model offers the opposite extreme. In this situation, most information-technology evaluations begin at the facilities. Although corporate may get involved to some extent, it is often the facility level's most senior manager who takes full profit responsibility for his business unit and justifies investments according to the specific needs of one site. Corporate information-technology staff likely exist but often serve as "traffic cops," who provide administrative support and coordination so that individual sites can share their experiences with others.

Most companies are actually a hybrid of both extreme business models. Much of the team-based emphasis of late has shifted the power of controlling information-technology strategy away from the corporate headquarters sites toward the individual facilities or business units. However, given the traditional power and strength of many of today's leading companies at the corporate headquarters level, this shift represents a better balance of control rather than an outright role reversal.

From an information-technology and simulation standpoint, a push system often creates greater exposure for new technologies to the entire enterprise. In many instances, if simulation is introduced at a corporate level in a push business model, there is a greater chance that it will succeed. This is because of the momentum, enthusiasm level, and early management buy-in that often occur when ideas flourish at "mission control." And, since strategic decisions often are made at a corporate level, the likelihood is greater that the initial project will have a significant impact and save a lot of money.

However, limitations can exist when simulation is introduced at a corporate level. In many circumstances, the technology is adopted by a corporate-level project team that makes the investment to facilitate a strategic project. For example, this may involve the construction of a new call center for handling customer-service calls. The incorporation of a simulation analysis in the strategic plan might help the company save $1 million. Yet the failure to retain a follow-on strategic project of the same magnitude may prevent the technology from spreading. The corporate-level project team may move on to an entirely different project rather than working to transfer the new technology to facilities throughout the organization. The team's new project might not involve simulation at all, and the initial momentum will subside.

When simulation is introduced at a facility level in a pull system, initially there is considerable enthusiasm for the new technology. Generally, a fair amount of internal selling takes place to get the first project off the ground (due in part to the cost of software and time, the fact that individuals have many competing projects, and the facility manager's short-term profit objectives). However, once the project gets started, it often succeeds because the entire simulation project team attack a model that they understand extremely well—their own facility. Data is easy to generate, many people in the business are responsive, and the project is completed in a timely fashion.

Unfortunately, the facility-level/pull scenario also has its shortcomings. If the successes of the individual facility are not made known to other sites and to corporate management, momentum and enthusiasm can be lost quickly. Or an enterprise may have various operations, which may or may not use simulation technology, depending upon the initiative demonstrated by individuals scattered throughout the firm. The company may fail to achieve any economy of scale in spreading its knowledge widely.

An additional issue to consider is that when simulation projects focus upon individual facilities, decisions may be made that are appropriate (perhaps optimal) for the individual site but are not appropriate for the entire enterprise. With a tremendous growth in enthusiasm for information-technology projects that examine the entire supply chain, a need exists for effective use of simulation across the entire business. As discussed in Chapter 5, supply-chain improvement or optimization cannot be accomplished fully without the use of simulation. An effective supply-chain simulation strategy typically requires a carefully coordinated initiative between a corporate team and the individual sites. Supply-chain projects tend to be push-initiated but should be coordinated with solid pull-oriented leadership.

▲ Push or Pull? . . . The Answer: A "Champion"

The spread of an emerging information technology throughout an enterprise can be enhanced dramatically by one or two "champions."

A "champion" works to educate management and other individuals who could benefit by simulation. In the early going, the champion helps to sell others internally on the idea of simulation. As simulation becomes adopted by the firm, he or she works to identify projects that can benefit from the technology. When simulation projects save money for the firm, the champion makes an effort to communicate the ROI broadly in order to accelerate the acceptance of the technology corporationwide. The champion becomes familiar with a simulation-software tool and becomes integrated with the simulation-project management methodology but does not necessarily become a primary simulation analyst himself. Rather, he may generate his best return for the company by finding ways for others to save money with simulation.

In a push system, the champion may travel to various facility sites in order to articulate the value of simulation, encouraging the individual business units or facilities to implement the technology. He may sponsor internal educational sessions for managers. Internal simulation newsletters and regular meetings of the entire corporate simulation user community also help the corporate-level simulation champion to grow and foster a simulation-aware culture throughout an organization.

In a pull system, a champion ordinarily fights his way up through the organizational hierarchy in order to proclaim the benefits of simulation. He may have been successful in the initial experience with simulation at his site, but if he truly wants his entire enterprise to consider simulation technology for all capital projects, he needs to raise the level of awareness aggressively. If his corporate staff is open to new suggestions (that is, assuming that the corporate team has people who can manage a simulation function), he could pursue that route. An alternative approach is for the facility-level champion gradually to introduce simulation to other facilities one-by-one. He may offer his own support to help sell the project and begin implementation so that he can deliberately build support for the new technology. After several sites are successfully deploying the technology, corporate staff may want to get involved.

The champion concept is typically required during an organization's early acceptance of simulation. At some point—often one or two years after the technology was first used successfully—simulation may settle in as an "accepted" tool for the entire enterprise. Several companies have established policies stating that capital appropriations greater than a certain amount of investment (say $50,000) must be simulated. In this case, simulation becomes part of the basic business-management concept. The cost-justification/rally-the-troops/sell-the-results cycle of the past becomes unnecessary as companies are positioned to reap the maximum benefit from simulation technology.

Typically, corporations whose project methodologies have matured use both the push and pull for managing simulation activity. A single person or a small group—often at corporate headquarters—serve to "police" the use of simulation. Often they establish simulation-project management methodologies and facilitate communication between simulation analysts throughout the firm. There may be a particularly skilled "expert" user at a centralized location who helps train and assist the facility-level users. However, most of the actual simulation-project work occurs at the facilities, where individuals who are closest to the business problems can focus on solving them via successful implementations.

Another variation occurs when individuals at a corporate central location build models that are turned over to the facilities to conduct analysis. Under this scenario, the corporate staff serve as consultants to sites in the field. Facility-level individuals may be trained on the value of simulation for problem solving and be given some direction for changing system conditions within the models; however, they do not actually build simulation models. This strategy may work well from the standpoint of developing a high simulation skill level at corporate headquarters; however, it compromises the potential benefit that facility-level individuals can derive from having to create a model of their own system. As stated in Chapter 3, simulation analysts often learn a tremendous amount about their operation while they are modeling it. Without giving facility-level individuals the chance to learn the entire simulation process, organizations are limiting the potential benefit that can be derived from enterprisewide simulation activity.

▲ Strategic versus Operational Usage

Much of this book has focused on the use of simulation for facilitating change in an "offline" fashion. In other words, the simulation model is not directly used by individuals who are managing the daily activities in the business application (i.e., shop floor, call center, etc.). When used in an offline fashion, only after the best possible scenario for the business was determined would the operating facility be affected by the results.

Chapter 3 briefly introduced the use of simulation for operational decision support. In Chapter 4, a few of the profiled companies shared experiences of successful operational use of simulation. This type of application presents an additional way for organizations to spread the use of simulation throughout their enterprises. Here, the technology is used on a weekly—or even daily—basis for making operational decisions.

The problem in using simulation only for facilitating offline strategic change is that strategic change does not occur as frequently as operational change. One facility may require a simulation analysis only once per year, which may not be enough to maintain substantial momentum for the technology. Using the technology on a regular basis offers opportunities both to realize ongoing savings and system improvements and to make the technology more visible. Increased visibility leads to more projects and consequently a greater return on your investment in simulation technology.

There is no reason why simulation models developed for aiding in strategic projects cannot be used to help to improve systems continually or evaluate ongoing changes to business conditions. The use of simulation as an operational tool provides you with the opportunity to fast-forward a current operation to the short-term or long-term future. In this context, decisions can be made today about issues that will affect the immediate future. Rather than simply accepting the business outcome that would occur normally, a facility manager making operational use of simulation can explore alternative—perhaps much better—solutions on a regular basis.

Companies in manufacturing are using simulation models daily and weekly to understand how their system will perform on a short-term basis. In these examples, a model exists of the current system environment, into which current orders and system status are automatically loaded. The model is then executed in order to understand the probable future behavior. For example, if you are using simulation in this context, you may determine that your factory will experience a bottleneck this Thursday that will force a key customer order to be late. To respond to this problem, you may decide to invest in overtime or juggle your order priorities to get the "hot one" out the door.

Simulation is particularly useful in an operational setting for manufacturing firms that practice the Theory of Constraints (TOC) approach to managing critical resources and bottlenecks. Often, external factors such as a sudden change in customer demand or market mix may cause a facility's bottleneck to shift to a new critical resource. A simulation model provides a means to anticipate this kind of problem and to alleviate it before it occurs. The Goldratt Institute (creator of TOC) uses simulation models as a teaching method for implementing an effective TOC strategy.

An additional example of the operational use of simulation would be the management of staff schedules in a package-delivery environment. In this case, a simulation model of an existing hub center and local delivery network would be used. The objective for each dispatch manager is to make certain that an adequate crew of truck drivers is working so that all packages are delivered by the end of the day. A file identifying all of the packages due for delivery on that day is entered into the simulation model. By running the model (taking into account all of the system variability), the dispatch manager determines the likelihood of getting all packages delivered with the current driver schedule. He may decide after running the model that it makes sense to schedule an additional driver to increase the chance of getting all packages delivered on time.

For companies to maximize their return on simulation technology, they should look for operational uses to go alongside the strategic initiatives. There is absolutely no reason that the ultimate "to-be" model should sit on the shelf after it has helped to design the system, when it can be used continually as an operational decision-support tool. By increasing the application domain of simulation, you can spread its use more widely and successfully throughout an enterprise.

7   Market Trends and the Future of Simulation

When there is no vision, the people perish.

PROVERBS

Over the next 20 years, computers will get a million times more powerful than they are today.

BILL GATES

In the information-technology business, we measure the "future" in months rather than years. Our time horizon for strategic decision making is typically 18 months or less. Trying to envision a tomorrow that is two or three years away is more akin to playing the lottery than anything that might be considered scientific or responsible. All-new technologies emerge on the scene at warp speed, setting new information-technology standards that were not even considered just a short time before.

Although they emerge quickly, new technologies may incubate slowly. They may take considerable time to develop and mature to the point where they are ready to appear on the mainstream market for millions of consumers. Notice, too, that intuitive and robust technologies that exude creativity and flair do not in and of themselves create mainstream markets. Consumer demand must also exist. This does not mean that customers specifically demand the new technology itself; rather, they demand the benefits that can be gained through the use of the new technology.

The combination of the maturation of new technology with a market base that quickly becomes aware of its benefits leads to the right mix of demand that can take a technology solution into the mainstream. This mix is taking place today with simulation. But to illustrate the situation, I would like to take you on a quick tour of how the most visible and successful information technology of this generation emerged into the mainstream. Let's take a look at the Internet.

A Case Study

From the Lab to the Mainstream

The advent of new technology can fundamentally change the way we do business. Yesterday, the fax machine was the latest tool transforming commerce. Imagine not being able to fax important documents to your colleagues and clients on a minute's notice. Today, the Internet is the technology that is changing the way we do business. And, though the phenomenal growth in its use began in 1992, it is a technology that was first conceived in 1969.

In 1969, the United States military wanted to be sure networked computers could talk to each other even if some of them were destroyed by a direct hit on a central point of control (perhaps by a nuclear weapon). The solution was created by the RAND Corporation, who devised a network architecture where each computer on the system would share the same responsibility as all the others. In September of '69 the network (known as TCP/IP) was successfully tested by four universities, and the Internet was born.

Internet technology grew at a steady pace in the 1970s and 1980s as university researchers under government contract used it to communicate and share information. In 1984, the National Science Foundation (NSF) built a network-architecture backbone for high-speed communication that helped propel the Internet further. However, at this time the 'Net was restricted for use only by the government, its contractors, and universities.

In 1989, Tim Berners-Lee created the Web at the European Laboratory for Particle Physics (CERN) near Geneva. He introduced the idea of hypertext linking of multiple documents for internal use at CERN. The approach worked extremely well, was eventually released to the Internet as a whole, and became the World Wide Web. In 1992, the first graphical user interface (Mosaic) was created by Marc Andreessen at the University of Illinois, making it much easier to use and access information on the Internet. That same year, commercial traffic found its way onto the Internet and the NSF backed down from policing the system. In 1994 and 1995, Netscape and Microsoft further advanced the user interface issue by releasing Internet browsers that could be conveniently integrated into PC desktop operating systems. These events allowed for the rapid explosion that makes today's Internet a mainstream part of most businesses in the civilized world.

By charting the Internet's growth from 1969 to today, we can cite various key events:

▼ 1969—TCP/IP network architecture created by RAND Corporation and Defense Advanced Research Projects Agency (DARPA) researchers, allowing cooperating computers to share resources across network

▼ 1975—TCP/IP network moves from experimentation phase to become operational (called ARPANET)

▼ 1980s—Increased investment by U.S. government (NSF, NASA, others)

▼ 1989—Creation of World Wide Web at CERN

▼ 1992—Creation of Mosaic at University of Illinois

▼ 1994/1995—Netscape and Microsoft release Internet browsers

▼ Today—Widespread acceptance by commercial world; dramatic growth in use

By 1992, the Internet had emerged as a technology for the mainstream. Its growth has been absolutely phenomenal. Figure 7-1 identifies the number of computers (referred to as hosts) connected to the Internet according to 1997 research conducted by Network Wizards (http://www.nw.com).

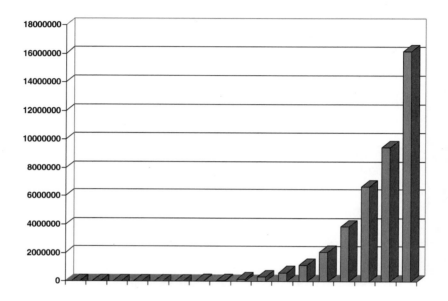

Figure 7-1 *Internet Host Computers*

O.K., back to planet Earth. I am certainly not suggesting that simulation technology will have the impact on commerce that the Internet has had. However, there are some intriguing parallels between the two technologies in terms of the paths they have followed before emerging into the mainstream. They both have experienced the following steps in the emergence of a new information-technology market:

▼ *First, a technology must be conceived, tried, and tested.* This happened with the Internet in 1969 and the early 1970s. With simulation, it occurred back in the 1960s.

▼ *Next, an early-adopting user community must prove it to be successful.* The Internet benefited from U.S. government and university users who were conducting research. Simulation also achieved its initial success in U.S. government and university research circles.

▼ *The technology itself must achieve dramatic ease of use and functional improvements.* The World Wide Web made the Internet more functional. Mosaic and new browsers have made it easier to use. Simulation software vendors have achieved major advances in both ease of use and functionality.

▼ *At the same time, surrounding information technology must advance to foster accelerated improvements that the new technology could not gain on its own.* The Internet leveraged the rapid growth of TCP/IP and is benefiting strongly today from advances in browsing technology and integration into operating systems such as Microsoft® Windows NT®. Simulation has benefited from faster PC's and better operating systems and is just beginning to leverage true integration with other mainstream technology solutions.

▼ *The commercial world must accept the technology and invest in it broadly.* This has occurred with the Internet in the 1990s. With simulation, it has just started to occur within the last few years.

In the case of the Internet, the rapid acceptance of the technology is due largely to the compelling benefits that its users recognize. For example, it saves time. It also saves money by avoiding long-distance phone calls and delivery charges for communicating information. And, now that it has been accepted on such a broad-scale basis, you have to have access to the Internet simply to deal with customers and fellow employees. You truly have no option but to become part of the market.

With simulation, the rapid growth of the market is occurring due to a variety of factors. Unlike the Internet, simulation technology is not a must-have vehicle for conducting basic business communication, so it must rely upon other market conditions to drive demand. The remainder of this chapter will focus on strong trends that are leading to rapid growth in market demand for simulation technology. When discussing each area, I will explain the effect the trend is having on the simulation market and user community today, where it is headed, and why this trend will lead to growth for the market. In doing so, I am not merely trying to convince you that simulation technology is emerging as a mainstream tool, I am aiming to share a vision that you can capitalize on—in a pragmatic way—to make your company more competitive by leveraging simulation technology to manage change.

▲ Trend #1—Simulation Is Aligning with Mainstream Desktop Technologies

The majority of the growth that the simulation market has experienced to date has been due to consistent progress in management awareness, software enhancements, and successful applications. Chapter 4 presented information, statistics, and "Simulation in Action" accounts that characterize this progress. Most of the simulation projects discussed in Chapter 4 were not integrated with other information-technology solutions.

As a stand-alone system, simulation can add tremendous value to business problem-solving projects. Integration of simulation with another information technology creates a synergy that increases the value of both. This integration also typically leads to a solution that is easier for a broad audience of users to exploit.

The leading simulation-software vendors in the market today are investing in technology and marketing integration with leading desktop-software companies in business diagramming, CAD, and activity-based costing technology. At the same time, the firms that have already been in the mainstream are seeking partnerships with smaller (but growing) simulation companies. The basic idea is to utilize existing desktop tools for what they do best (i.e., create flowcharts and animation layouts, and organize information) while using simulation alongside for dynamic business modeling. Integration of simulation with complementary desktop technology provides several compelling benefits to the user community:

▼ It decreases simulation–model development time. For example, if a facility has already been created in a CAD system and if facility processes have been represented in a business-diagramming solution, this work may not have to be reproduced in a simulation tool.

▼ It simplifies the process of making changes to model information. Changing values of information in a spreadsheet may be easier than doing the same within a simulation tool.

▼ It increases the usability of simulation technology across an enterprise. Since many users are already familiar with mainstream desktop tools, they become more comfortable with adding simulation to their desktop-technology toolbox.

More than ever before, corporations evaluating simulation technology are placing a very high weighting on the tool's ability to integrate with desktop solutions. As this trend continues, more software vendors are focusing on this area of technology integration and are forming business partnerships to create joint-selling opportunities.

▲ The Future

For the future, a number of outcomes are possible. First, we may find vendors that have traditionally been leaders in mainstream markets entering the simulation market as a natural growth of their business. The opportunity to take a static system representation and add business dynamics may represent a significant new business opportunity. They may do this as a strategy to offer an additional product or as a way to add value to an existing product (for example, a business-diagramming software vendor may make simulation of static flowcharts a compelling product feature).

At a minimum, key software vendors that sell established mainstream products will strategically align with simulation-software vendors to produce highly integrated solutions. From a user perspective, the complementary technologies will be so fused that little or no effort will be required to move between applications. The use of ActiveX™ and Object Linking and Embedding (OLE) technologies will provide the foundation for dramatic improvements in this area.

Clearly, the widespread integration of simulation technology with other desktop technologies will continue to drive a dramatic increase in use. I predict that this trend will intensify over the next few years and that those vendors who most fully exploit opportunities in this area will earn a large share of the overall simulation market.

Trend #2—Organizations Are Developing a Strategy for Using Simulation Across the Enterprise

In the past, companies would use simulation for facilitating significant changes, but only when they had ample time to utilize the technology. Most of the projects were focused on manufacturing problems. Very little simulation analysis was done of warehousing, distribution, or supply-chain applications. Even in manufacturing, only a small percentage of the overall number of candidate projects were modeled, owing in part to the steep learning curve in using the software and a lack of management enthusiasm for the technology.

Today, simulation is being implemented across the enterprise. In Chapter 4, I shared several stories of how this is occurring. Today's leading corporations are teaching new managers the value of simulation technology. Some require its use as a standard procedure in support of new capital investment decisions. The result is that companies are gaining much greater return on their investment in simulation across the enterprise.

The success of simulation across an entire corporation can be attributed to many factors. For example, as companies grow their usage of and investment in simulation, they are addressing a much broader collection of applications. I have already discussed many other reasons why the simulation market is emerging (easier-to-use software, PC advances, etc.); however, I have yet to discuss the trend within organizations to create a corporate methodology for utilizing this technology. Many companies have established—often via the use of a "champion"—a set of procedures for successfully applying simulation technology. Internal procedures for utilizing simulation are well documented. Training courses are made available to newcomers to the technology, and, in many companies, internal user groups of simulation analysts have formed to share models and project information.

An additional component of the new corporate simulation methodology has been the increased sharing of completed simulation models in a "run-time" mode. Here, individuals who are creating models of business processes can pass along a completed application for others to perform the "what-if" analysis. Persons receiving simulation models of factories, warehouses, or call centers are able to explore varying business scenarios by simply changing numbers in a spreadsheet or other easy-to-access user interface. Salespersons in the field can explore the impact of a new customer order on an existing system by inputting the order quantity and running a model. This "run-time" model concept places much of the value of simulation in the hands of a much broader audience.

▲ The Future

In the future, the ratio of nonmanufacturing applications to manufacturing will continue to rise. The potential in such application areas as logistics, warehousing, and distribution is only beginning to be realized. The growing diversity in applications will lead to broader exposure for the technology, in general, which ultimately leads to real market growth.

Corporatewide implementation of simulation technology in the future may involve the use of corporate intranets for model and methodology sharing. This is just starting to take place and will continue to expand in the next several years. Under this scenario, the intranet server becomes a repository of models that can be used across the firm. If the organization has consistent operating procedures for managing a call center or distribution center, a model that has been constructed for a specific center can be reused when designing a new one. In fact, "what-if" scenarios can be explored across the intranet, eliminating the need for remote facilities to even install simulation software on their local PC's. Organizations using animated models for communicating to customers can dial into their own intranet while at the customers' site to present recommendations and explore alternatives.

Self-learning simulation courses will be easily downloaded from corporate intranets in the future. Courses will teach effective simulation methodology (perhaps as described in Chapter 6) as well as how to use simulation software. Training courses will feature workshops that are directly relevant to the company with example models taken from real-world projects. A history of modeling projects will be maintained for analysts on the company intranet.

Management consulting firms will use intranets as a means for sharing client information throughout their practice. Analysts engaged on a project for a semiconductor firm in Tokyo can access simulation models created for a different client in San Jose to learn more about the industry process. Rather than simply exploring research notes that a fellow consultant may have entered in a database, using an actual simulation of the business process located on an intranet server will add tremendously to the management consulting firm's overall knowledge base.

Concurrently, significant advances will occur within the simulation-software community to create ActiveX™ components and/or Java applets for sharing simulation technology. New simulation components will be integrated on World Wide Web sites, intranets, and other client/server environments. This technology will affect integration of simulation with both desktop and enterprise (e.g., ERP) applications, leading to new ways of performing business process analysis.

Trend #3—Simulation Is Becoming a Critical Module in Transaction-Focused Enterprise-Level ▲ Software Systems

In Chapter 5, I discussed the role of simulation relative to enterprise-level technologies such as enterprise resource-planning (ERP) systems and workflow-management software. Here, I differentiate these technologies from the desktop described above in that they typically take on a more strategic role than, for example, the spreadsheet. They are also used operationally for processing all key business transactions. Companies invest in ERP and workflow-management technology in building an information-technology backbone for management of day-in, day-out business. Installations of these technologies (including associated consulting fees) often cost in the millions of dollars, with implementations taking many months, or frequently years.

Consulting firms and some large organizations are beginning to integrate simulation technology with their enterprise-level solutions. Software vendors who supply ERP and workflow-management technology have either started to partner with simulation-technology vendors or at least claim they will have a simulation-enabled solution in the near future. Simulation, when used alongside these enterprise-level systems, is valuable for conducting short-term look-aheads and performing offline "what-if" analysis. Simulation also adds value in that it facilitates the testing of systems proposed for enterprise-level implementation *before* the business goes online with ERP or workflow management.

▲ The Future

ERP software firms will exploit simulation technology as an integrated methodology within their software and consulting-services practice. This may occur via an alliance with simulation-software companies or by developing new software solutions internally. New ERP engagements will rely upon simulation technology early in the process in order to specify efficient business process configurations. Once the business process layout has been identified, an ERP application can be adapted to serve as its transaction-processing system. ERP applications that conform to a less-than-ideal business configuration will be avoided. (Unfortunately, today millions of dollars in ERP implementations are aimed at business configurations that could benefit from dramatic change.)

When fully operational, ERP systems will provide a "look-ahead" option, where a simulation model of the business can be executed and manipulated for process improvements. This model will be a replica of the ERP-driven system and will not interfere with the current procedures that take place in the business. Once changes have been explored and accepted within the simulation environment, they can be communicated to the ERP system in an automatic way. The ERP system will accept updated information from the simulation model and continue processing.

Workflow-management systems will leverage simulation technology in a way that is directly analogous to ERP. As with ERP, the use of simulation will reduce the risk of faulty implementations and will serve as an effective offline analyzer of better business decisions. When ERP and workflow-management software vendors and consultants begin relying upon simulation as a standard value-added module, demand for simulation technology will increase—driving market growth.

Trend #4—The "BPR Craze" Is Driving the Need for Simulation

When first exposed to what I refer to as the "BPR craze," I assumed that business process reengineering was a marketing gimmick, conceived by management consultants as a concept around which they could invent expensive service solutions for senior corporate management. After learning more about the concept and watching the market mature, I no longer view BPR in this light.

Hammer and Champy first placed BPR on the map with their book *Reengineering the Corporation* (1993), in which a systematic methodology for conducting organizational process redesign was introduced. Since then, many consultants, software vendors, and large enterprises have created the "science" of BPR. Various specific modeling orientations, such as IDEF0 (founded by the U.S. government), Unified Modeling Language (UML) activity diagrams, and Rummler-Brache swim diagrams, have emerged as standard ways to depict business processes and their many relationships. Each of these BPR process-description methodologies (and several others) can be researched easily on the Internet. They are all focused on making it easy to model business applications at varying levels, where high-level business processes (sometimes referred to as "parents") are composed of underlying subprocesses ("children"). Individuals can create models of entire business configurations using these methodologies.

Nearly all BPR "modeling" is focused on capturing a static depiction of a business setting. Static models of "as-is" systems can be compared against models of "to-be" configurations. However, without the ability to run the model in a dynamic way, it is nearly impossible to determine which "to-be" scenario is in fact the best. This is why simulation is extremely valuable when conducting BPR initiatives.

The "BPR craze" has already had a profound effect on the simulation market. Many new software products have emerged on the scene in response to the new demand. As stated in Chapter 4, Gartner Group recognizes the growing utility of simulation for BPR initiatives and predicts that 20% of all BPR projects will take advantage of simulation by the year 1998—a substantial growth achieved primarily in the last two years.

▲ The Future

Gartner Group's prediction will come to pass, and additional momentum for the successful application of simulation for BPR projects will be gained. An additional Gartner Group prediction— that 80% of all BPR tools will provide simulation capability (directly or via interface) by the year 2000—also will occur.

Eventually, BPR projects will be conducted with simulation as a standard component of the study. "To-be" systems will not be identified without some form of simulation-based treatment of business dynamics. The widespread demand for simulation technology by BPR analysts will affect the simulation-software market in several ways:

▼ In some cases, BPR-focused simulation-software products will be used.

▼ In other cases, simulation-software vendors that serve broad markets will add functionality to their tools to address BPR methodologies.

▼ Workflow management-software vendors will become more competitive in BPR circles by integrating simulation technology with their products.

Some management consulting firms and large organizations will cut against the current BPR grain by insisting that Rummler–Brache, IDEF0, and related methodologies are tedious (too structured and often difficult to understand) and that basic business process flowcharts are more manageable and appropriate for conducting business process redesign. This move threatens to weaken the "science" of BPR, removing the methodological processes of depicting business applications that have been standardized in some circles. Some leading firms may coin their own proprietary approaches for business process management and analysis. Will these approaches still be known to the world as BPR, or will BPR fall by the wayside as a fad of the 90s? I cannot answer this question. I will say, however, that the demand for simulation technology the "BPR craze" has created is substantial and will continue to grow. It has already caused market growth for simulation and will continue to do so for some time to come. Other proprietary approaches to business process redesign will likely utilize simulation as well, since they still need a way to facilitate the transition between "as-is" and "to-be" while considering the dynamics of business problems.

Trend #5—Supply-Chain Applications Require Simulation

To marry the term "BPR" with "craze" and not do the same for "supply chain" may be inappropriate. Clearly, many respected management consulting firms and leading corporations have placed a strategic emphasis on analyzing business processes across the entire enterprise rather than simply "inside the walls" of a manufacturing or warehouse operation. I'll omit the "craze" handle only because supply-chain projects date back quite some time. It's just that the intensity and momentum that have placed the concept front-and-center in our lives have peaked here in the 1990s.

Organizations are facilitating very strategic decisions through successful supply-chain analysis projects. For example, Levi Strauss is in the midst of a dramatic change in its entire distribution strategy (from a primarily national strategy to a largely regional approach) in order to improve customer service and gain efficiencies in transportation costs. Companies are more commonly viewing their specific business facilities as critical pieces in an organizational puzzle rather than merely as stand-alone operations. In this new way of thinking, the challenge often becomes to focus first on implementing (via relocation, new construction, and/or acquisition, if necessary) the best supply-chain strategy *and then* to optimize the individual components of the corporate collection. As suggested in Chapter 5, there is some risk in creating an "ideal" facility configuration that does not serve the best interests of the aggregate business.

Levi Strauss and many other of the world's leading firms (you might recall the Motorola story in Chapter 4) are using simulation technology effectively for supply-chain management. Given the many millions of actions that occur within a business, it is not responsible to think of making decisions without some consideration for the system dynamics that exist throughout.

Software vendors are lining up to capitalize on the new supply-chain emotion. Several companies (i2 Technologies, Manugistics, and CAPS Logistics, to name a few) now offer supply-chain technologies that have become very successful. These are typically optimization technologies similar to those I described in Chapter 5. Optimization vendors are growing at phenomenal rates and are poised to become major players in the information-technology business in the very near future. Unfortunately, at the time of this writing, no supply-chain software vendor has truly integrated simulation (as defined in this book) into its supply-chain solution. This will change.

▲ The Future

The simulation market will benefit from today's supply-chain enthusiasm in two distinct ways. One is that simulation will be used more and more often as a stand-alone technology for successful supply-chain analysis. As companies continue to communicate their successes to others (including their suppliers), more corporate buy-in will occur. In addition to the leverage simulation technology will gain from one successful supply-chain application referencing the next, the market will also gain support from those who are already practicing simulation within individual facilities. Individuals like John Liang at Motorola, who have been successful in applying simulation for facility-level projects, will champion the use of the technology for analyzing the supply chain. Corporate executives who have been affected by the emotion of supply-chain analysis will receive these champions with an open mind, leading to increased awareness and investment in simulation.

A further stimulus to the growth of simulation technology is that the supply-chain optimization vendors will either partner with leading simulation firms or create their own simulation-technology solutions in an integrated fashion with their supply-chain optimization systems. This will occur for several reasons. First, simulation adds value to supply-chain optimization systems, since it truly allows analysts to account for system dynamics. Second, the customers of these vendors will soon require such an integration; the availability of simulation for dynamic system depiction will become a requirement for winning new business and for successful project implementations. Finally, the marginal profits that can be generated via the addition of a value-added technology (and associated services) will motivate today's leading supply-chain vendors to add simulation to their technology arsenals.

▬ Trend #6—Simulation Adds Value to ▲ Scheduling Solutions

The idea of scheduling a manufacturing, call-center, or airline ticket-counter staffing operation without the use of information technology is, for the most part, behind us. While some smaller firms are only today upgrading to basic computer-based scheduling tools, most of the progressive world takes advantage of computer hardware and software to run their operations.

Today, even the computer-based scheduling often found in traditional MRP II systems is not enough. Traditional MRP-based tools do not account for resource-capacity restrictions. In other words, they will assume that orders can be manufactured regardless of the existence of sufficient capacity (i.e., machines, operators, and material handling equipment). This shortcoming has led to the emergence of finite-capacity scheduling technology in the 1990s.

Today, many leading scheduling-software vendors are turning to simulation technology as a way to improve accuracy. Simulation-based scheduling offers a compelling advantage over both traditional scheduling and modern finite-capacity scheduling technology since it is typically able to create higher-quality schedules (as discussed in Chapter 5).

Significant improvements in the technology are necessary to guarantee increased growth and usage of simulation-based scheduling. Traditional stand-alone simulation-software tools lack many key features required by scheduling applications (e.g., interface to ERP systems, Gantt charts, tardiness reports, etc.), and traditional scheduling solutions with added simulation technology lack the robustness of quality simulation engines.

▲ The Future

Over the next few years, we will see a dramatic increase in the application of simulation technology to scheduling as the benefits of this technology become more widely understood and accepted. As software vendors in the simulation and scheduling marketplace continue to incorporate the strengths of the two technologies into integrated solutions, organizations will benefit from easier-to-use, more robust technology.

Simulation-based scheduling tools will be deployed as part of broader ERP system architectures as well. The current trend within the ERP community has been to offer a basic scheduling module as part of their standard solution while offering additional options for finite-capacity and simulation-based scheduling via technology partnerships with other organizations. As more successful applications go online supported by simulation-based scheduling, the technology will become a standard component of an ERP implementation rather than an option that is not fully understood by the market.

Trend #7—Market Verticalization Helps Decrease Learning Curve, Increase Usage

As information-technology markets mature, software vendors invest in making their solutions more robust and easier to use. Product features are added to accommodate the specific needs of customers. Graphical user interfaces (GUIs) are continually improved to help drive down the software learning curve. As a technology becomes more intuitive, more practitioners can take advantage of it and the market grows. One way that information-technology vendors extend the usability and usefulness of their solutions is by creating versions of their technology aimed at specific vertical markets. Examples of this surround us. TurboTax®, the best-selling tax-return preparation software, is available in a standard form for personal use and as TurboTax® Business for preparing small-business returns. Of course, the products are very similar in many ways; however, the business version of the product offers features and reports tailored specifically to the needs of the business owner. It has been verticalized to address the needs of a specific user community.

Most traditional simulation-software tools employ a collection of general modeling features. Although the modeling tools were designed to be general-purpose (i.e, nonvertical) modeling systems, they typically had some focus on manufacturing applications. As discussed in Chapter 4, the manufacturing sector has been a driving force in the growth of simulation, and this has influenced the design of most of the general-purpose simulation modeling tools. Today, however, vertical-market simulation solutions are appearing on the scene at a growing pace. In recent years, there has been dramatic growth in the application of simulation in nonmanufacturing areas such as health care systems, transportation systems, communication systems, packaging systems, and BPR. Although in the past these applications have been modeled using general-purpose tools created for the manufacturing market, the trend is toward having dedicated simulation tools for each of the primary vertical application areas.

A vertical simulation tool has some significant advantages over a general-purpose modeling tool. Because it has features that are focused on the problems as well as terminology of the target market, it is easier to learn and use, and simulation projects can typically be completed in much less time. One of the important new technology developments that has facilitated this trend is the introduction of template-based simulation tools. In these, the modeling constructs are not hard-coded into the software, but instead are soft-specified within a separate modeling template. New templates can be created quickly for new vertical applications without requiring the complete development of a new simulation modeling tool for each vertical application.

▲ The Future

More vertical simulation tools will appear on the scene. The rapid increase in their number will be abetted by template-based simulation tools and object-oriented technology, which makes it easier for firms to create them. New tools will be created for yet untapped vertical-market areas, and better solutions will be released for those areas where current simulation technology has not yet reached its potential.

Most vertical-market solutions available today were created by simulation-software vendors; however, as these same vendors deliver technology to market that allows end-users and third parties to create their own vertical solutions quickly and easily, the market will recognize even greater leverage. For example, an automotive firm may opt to invest in the creation of simulation tools that are vertically focused on welding lines, paint lines, or parts distribution. While these tools may not be sold to other firms, they achieve the same objective as "off-the-shelf" vertical technology in that they improve the tool's focus on specific problems, decrease the associated learning curve, and shorten the simulation-project completion time.

Other approaches for achieving verticalization will also help the market expand. For example, as simulation-software products continue to improve in the area of integration with other technologies, broad decision-support applications that have simulation technology embedded within them can be offered for specific vertical markets. An example would be a solution for managing call centers that integrated simulation, forecasting, and scheduling in one environment. Here, the overall solution may be more vertically focused than its components. This can be achieved by creating a high-level, focused GUI that automatically sends appropriate information to the component technologies. This interface may be created using Microsoft® Visual Basic® for Applications or other development environments.

◼ Trend #8–Simulation Models Facilitate Buyer/ ◣ Supplier Relationships

As many large organizations increase their commitment to simulation technology for change management, they are beginning to require their supplier community to follow suit. Mandating the technology for supplier projects helps to facilitate communication between the firms during the sales and manufacturing processes. Simulation can also give confidence to the buyer that a cost-effective strategy was utilized for making products, building a new facility, or for delivering a service. It allows the buyer to participate in exploring various "what-if" alternatives involving delivery and cost tradeoffs. Many large firms also require a completed simulation model as part of the deliverable from suppliers. This model may be particularly useful when the buying organization wishes to apply simulation technology itself. For example, if the supplier is providing equipment, a model representing how the equipment performs can be reused by the buyer within a larger simulation application of an entire manufacturing facility.

The fact that large organizations in the automotive, electronics, and aerospace industries are mandating the use of simulation technology is driving market growth. Companies that might not have embraced simulation so quickly are being driven to do so simply to win (and/or protect) business relationships. The investment is initially forced, but it often leads to a positive return for the supplier organization that begins recognizing the value of the technology for broad application areas.

▲ The Future

In the near term, larger firms will continue to require that simulation be used as part of supplier projects. This trend—which exists primarily today in manufacturing industries—will extend to many other areas, such as construction and call-center outsourcing. At the same time, many suppliers will begin to use simulation technology more proactively as a way to differentiate themselves. By utilizing simulation technology, suppliers can claim that they are implementing the best manufacturing or service methodology, which leads to savings and value for customers. In some cases, this strategy of selling simulation as part of a total supplier solution will drive the acceptance of simulation from the supplier to the buyer. It will also force other suppliers to embrace the technology for competitive reasons.

Equipment vendors will also increase their use of simulation technology for sales and value-added reasons. Animated models help vendors sell systems. Simulation will allow systems integrators to work in concert with customers to specify resource requirements for all-new facilities. As object-oriented technology grows in acceptance and application, equipment vendors can deliver simulation objects that match the functionality of their robots, welders, conveyors, and other products. These objects can simply be "plugged in" to simulation-software solutions for rapid model development. As suppliers offer simulation-enabled solutions, they will drive the need for such technology by the buyer community, thereby driving market growth for simulation technology in general.

Trend #9—Simulation Can Be Used to Control Manufacturing Systems

I am constantly amazed by the amount of money invested by manufacturing organizations to have custom control logic written to run their automated facilities. Welding machines, cranes, various automated assembly machines, and automated guided vehicles (AGV's) are typically controlled by software programs that send instructions via programmable logic controllers (PLC's) to the shop floor. According to a research study conducted by the U.S. Department of Defense, roughly 50% of the average investment in a new manufacturing facility is directed at fees to have custom control software developed for the factory.

A new and growing area for simulation technology is in real-time applications. Much of the exact system logic that must be created (coded) for control systems exists within a simulation model of the same factory. In this context, the simulation model is used to control a real system. For real-time applications, the simulation model is purposely slowed down to run in real time and to execute in parallel to the real system. During execution, the model exchanges messages with either a PLC or a person on the shop floor. These messages allow the model and real system to remain synchronized. These messages are also used by the model to issue commands to the real system to initiate specific tasks.

A simulation-based control system has a number of important advantages over traditional control systems. One very important advantage is that it can, at any point in time, use its system model to examine the system status at some time in the future. In a manufacturing application, for example, we could use the simulation-based control system to predict the status of the facility at any time in the future. In addition, by leveraging the decision logic that we have already built into our simulation model, we can dramatically reduce the complexity of the control software that must be developed for our facility.

▲ The Future

The rate of growth in acceptance of simulation technology for controlling manufacturing will lag that for other areas discussed in this chapter. While some organizations, such as several U.S. defense contractors, have already embraced this technology, significant advancement in capability and integration features is required before this application area matures and drives real market growth for simulation.

One likely outcome in the next few years is that manufacturing execution system (MES) vendors (such as Intellution and FASTech) and PLC vendors (such as Allen Bradley) will integrate simulation technology with their technology solutions. The addition of simulation-based control systems will add value to their technologies for better decision support and for differentiation in selling against vendors that do not have a simulation-enabled offering. This integration may occur via partnership with simulation-technology vendors or as new development efforts by the MES and PLC market players.

▲ Trend #10—The Emergence of Market Leaders

If you look back on new information-technology markets over the past 20 years, you can typically identify a small group of companies that helped lead their respective industries to the mainstream. For example, Lotus dominated the early spreadsheet market. IBM was (and is) the clear leader in the mainframe business. In the personal operating systems market, Microsoft and IBM battled with Apple until Microsoft emerged as the dominant player. The point is that emerging markets need market leaders with vision and tenacity to help entire industries emerge. In simulation today, the market remains fragmented. There are at least 100 software vendors touting some form of simulation solution.

While a few of the players are more established than others, no single firm has as much as a one-third share of the simulation market, with most firms owning a very small percentage of the overall space. It is very important for the overall growth of the simulation market that a leader (or small group of leaders) emerge from the pack. According to Geoffrey Moore's *Crossing the Chasm*, mainstream markets want to do business with known market leaders. Enterprises that invest heavily in the technology need to partner with vendors that not only will be in business for the long haul but will serve as the visionaries to create the products and market of tomorrow.

▲ The Future

I predict that as the simulation market grows rapidly in the late 1990s and early 21st century, one to three players will emerge as clear market leaders. I have no doubt that the market will create a small number of dominant players. Whether this occurs via rapid growth of the existing simulation firms (perhaps through a successful initial public offering) or via merger and/or acquisition is difficult to say. The key is for one or more companies to gain the size and required critical mass to fully capitalize on—and in fact, *drive*—the growth of the market into the next century. In order to do this, the leading company (or companies) will need the financial strength to invest aggressively in technology, marketing, and partnering to fully exploit the potential that exists for rapid growth of the market.

◼ The Future of Simulation—Final Comments

The traditional simulation market has grown at a modest pace for the past 20 years largely via intensive selling by simulation vendors and the corporate champions who have shared their simulation experiences and helped to spread its use across their firms. The rate of growth accelerated in the early 1990s, and the technology has established itself as an exciting market for the future. For the many reasons cited in this closing chapter, market conditions are beginning to gel today that are driving a dramatic increase in need for simulation technology. Much as the Internet was able to leverage technologies such as the World Wide Web and Internet browser software, the simulation market will leverage other technologies—as well as market trends such as BPR and supply-chain initiatives—to achieve a new level of strategic significance in the future.

My strong conviction is that the simulation market will become at least a billion dollars in size by the year 2000. The challenge that you now have before you is not so much to identify *if* you will become part of this growth, but rather *when* you will and *how* you should leverage its emergence to your strategic advantage. If you are not currently taking advantage of simulation technology within your organization, making the move to do so *now* may represent one of the best changes that you will ever have the opportunity to manage.

References

Champy, James, and Michael Hammer, *Reengineering the Corporation: A Manifesto for Business Revolution*, HarperBusiness, New York, 1993.

Drucker, Peter, *The Practice of Management*, Harper & Row, Publisher, Inc., New York, 1954.

Empey, Charlotte, Visio Corporation market research on business diagramming, 1997.

Excellence in Practice: Innovation and Excellence in Workflow and Imaging, Future Strategies Inc., 1997.

Goldratt, Eliyahu M., *The Goal*, North River Press, Great Barrington, MA, 1984.

Harrington, J. H., *Business Process Improvement: The Breakthrough Strategy for Total Quality, Productivity, and Competitiveness*, McGraw-Hill, New York, 1991.

Kleinberg, Ken, *BPR Simulation Market Research Notes*, Stamford, CT, March 1997.

Michel, Roberto, "Simulating Conversation," *Manufacturing Systems*, March 1997.

Michel, Roberto, "The Heart of the Matter," *Manufacturing Systems*, April 1997.

Moore, Geoffrey A., *Crossing the Chasm*, HarperBusiness, New York, 1991.

Next-Generation Manufacturing: A Framework for Action, Bethlehem, PA, November 1996.

Parker, Kevin, "Build to Plan, Schedule to Order," *Manufacturing Systems*, February 1997.

Phillips, William D., *Report of the National Critical Technologies Panel*, National Critical Technologies Panel, Arlington, VA, March 1991.

Polito, Joe, Hank Grant, and Al Jones, *Enterprise Integration: A Tool's Perspective*, Kluwer Academic Publishers, Norwell, MA, 1994.

Ravindran, A., Don T. Phillips, and James J. Solberg, *Operations Research: Principles and Practice*, John Wiley & Sons, New York, 1987.

Selected World Development Indicators, World Development Report, Washington, DC, June 1997.

Sterne, Jim, *World Wide Web Marketing*, John Wiley & Sons, Inc., New York, 1996.

Tate, Austin, *The Evolution of Workflow and other research notes*, Workflow Management Coalition, Brussels, Belgium, 1997.

Turbide, David, "Why We're Here," *Midrange ERP*, January/February 1997.

Index

193